Small Wonder

Small

THE LITTLE RED SCHOOLHOUSE

YALE UNIVERSITY PRESS   NEW HAVEN & LONDON

Wonder

IN HISTORY AND MEMORY

Jonathan Zimmerman

Published with assistance from the foundation established in memory of
William McKean Brown.

Jane Kenyon, "Trouble with Math in a One-Room Country School,"
copyright © 2005 by the Estate of Jane Kenyon. Reprinted from *Collected
Poems* with the permission of Graywolf Press, Saint Paul, Minnesota.

Joyce Carol Oates, "Nostalgia," from *Tenderness* (1996), copyright © 1996 by
The Ontario Review, Inc. Reprinted with permission.

Set in Janson type by Integrated Publishing Solutions, Grand Rapids, MI.

Printed in the United States of America by Vail-Ballou Press, Binghamton, NY.

Library of Congress Cataloging-in-Publication Data
Zimmerman, Jonathan, 1961–
Small wonder : the little red schoolhouse in history and
memory / Jonathan Zimmerman.
p. cm.—(Icons of America)
Includes bibliographical references and index.
ISBN 978-0-300-12326-5 (alk. paper)
1. School buildings—Social aspects—United States—History. I. Title.
LB3218.A1Z56 2009
371.6'20973—dc22   2008020367

A catalogue record for this book is available from the British Library.

This paper meets the requirements of ANSI/NISO Z39.48–1992
(Permanence of Paper).
It contains 30 percent postconsumer waste (PCW) and is certified by the For-
est Stewardship Council (FSC).

10 9 8 7 6 5 4 3 2 1

For Rose A. Zimmerman
See you on Tuesday

Contents

Contents

Acknowledgments

Like babies, some books take a long time to be born. This one arrived rather quickly, thanks to the skilled midwifery of several friends and colleagues. I am especially grateful to Mark Crispin Miller, editor of the Icons of America series at Yale University Press, for asking me to write for the series. Thanks also to Richard Arum and Michael Carroll, who encouraged me to accept the invitation when my own spirit was wavering.

Fellow historians Jeffrey Mirel and John Rury read the first draft of this book with scholarly care, offering excellent suggestions for improving it. Thanks also to Emma Fletcher and Kate Scherer at Fletcher and Parry LLC, who brought the book to Yale; to editorial director Jonathan Brent, who has supported the project from the start; to Annelise Finegan, who shepherded it through revision and production; and to Susan Laity, who provided expert copyediting and good cheer. Finally, Jill Krupnik did heroic spadework in obtaining copies of my illustrations and permissions to reproduce them.

At New York University's Steinhardt School of Culture, Education, and Human Development, Deans Mary Brabeck and Ron Robin have been steady advocates and true friends. The same goes for many other colleagues at NYU, too numerous to list here. But thanks especially to René Arcilla, who gracefully shouldered the burdens of chairing my department while I shuffled off to write this book. To me, René epitomizes the values that any university is supposed to teach: integrity, curiosity, and humility. I am grateful for his friendship and example.

I am also grateful to several new colleagues at New York University's program in Ghana, where I completed work on this project. Akosua Anyidoho, Marian Ansa-Otu, Anthoniette Taylor, Christa Sanders, and Victor Yeboah have all been kind guides to this wonderful country. I hope they will come visit us in America sometime, so that we can reciprocate their hospitality.

Susan Coffin has been my loving companion on this adventure, and on all the others. We feel fortunate to share it with our daughters, Sarah and Rebecca, who have faced the challenges of overseas life with grace and grit. We are proud to be their parents.

The hardest part of going away was leaving my grandmother, Rose Aginsky Zimmerman. Thanks to Joan Malczewski and Sydney LaStella for looking after her while we were gone. And thanks most of all to Grandma, whose century on earth has enlivened us all. This book is for her, and for all of our Tuesday nights together.

Introduction

On 11 April 2002, the U.S. Department of Education held a rally at its Washington, D.C., headquarters to celebrate its signature reform measure, No Child Left Behind. Community activists, students, and even local football star Darrell Green paid tribute to the new federal law. Secretary of Education Rod Paige unveiled the eight new entrances to the department's headquarters, built to protect passersby during renovations to the building's facade. Each one was shaped to resemble America's most enduring educational symbol: the little red schoolhouse. Like so many other renditions of the icon, each entrance bore a slanted roof and a bell tower; the only new element was the name of the schoolhouse, "No Child Left Behind," which was starkly emblazoned across the front. "We serve the ideal of the little red schoolhouse," Paige told the rally. "It is one of the greatest symbols of America—a symbol that every child must be taught and every child must learn, that every community was involved and every parent's input valued. Those little schoolhouses were built to serve a need: to equip children as citizens and workers." As the new entrances suggested, No Child Left Behind would do the same. Invoking the best of America's past, it would prepare us for an even brighter future.[1]

Yet critics of the measure summoned the Little Red Schoolhouse *against* No Child Left Behind, claiming that the new law assaulted long-standing traditions of local control. In a 2006 television advertisement, for example, North Carolina county school board candidate Christopher Knight portrayed a little red schoolhouse under attack from the Death Star space station of the popular *Star Wars* film series. "When it comes to education, government bureaucracy is like a cosmic bully," a voice-over warned. "Legislation like No Child Left Behind is targeting and destroying our ability to best teach our children." Then the thirty-two-year-old Knight appeared, brandishing the same type of light saber that Luke Skywalker used to vanquish his enemies. "I believe in local control over our own schools, because I have more than enough faith in the parents and teachers of Rockingham County," Knight declared. Knight went down to defeat in the November 2006 elections, but his advertisement developed a small cult following; by April 2008, it had been watched more than two hundred thousand times on YouTube.[2]

Despite their differences, Rod Paige and Christopher Knight could agree upon one thing: the importance of the little red schoolhouse itself. So does the rest of the country. Whatever their political or cultural orientations, whatever their race or class or ethnicity, Americans use a remarkably consistent icon to symbolize their diverse educational institutions. A century ago, most American students attended a one-room school; today, almost nobody does. But *images* of the little red schoolhouse—its roof, its bell, its flag, and most of all its color—are ubiquitous, instantly recognizable to anyone who reads a newspaper, watches television, or shops on the Internet. The cyber-auction Web site eBay listed fifty-four different items for sale in August 2007 that bore a little red schoolhouse theme, including school-shaped Christmas tree ornaments, birdhouses, clocks, quilting patterns, and jewelry. "Red school house with a bell tower," read the description for a silver-and-enamel charm, which sold for $12.88. "Don't be tardy to class! Great for teachers and students." The previous month, the *Philadelphia Inquirer* published a cartoon to accompany a plea for more state funds for the city's ailing public schools. All the cartoonist needed to draw was a bell tower and flag atop the map of Pennsylvania, with a dollar sign locating Philadelphia on the map. Readers could figure out the rest.[3]

This book tells the story of how—and why—the little red schoolhouse became an American icon, shared and beloved by all. Amid the industrial boom of the late 1800s, poets started to celebrate the one-room school as the locus of America's lost rural simplicity; artists painted it red, even though most real schools were white or gray. Single-teacher schools came under fire at the turn of the century from self-described progressive reformers, who sought to replace them with larger, consolidated institutions. They also took aim at the sentimentalism surrounding the one-room school, exposing the wide gaps between its romantic image and its harsh reality. Into the Great Depression, liberal muckrakers and photographers portrayed the rural one-room school as the ultimate emblem of American poverty and inequality. But these criticisms melted away during World War II and the Cold War, when the little red schoolhouse began to symbolize America's timeless democratic heritage in the face of its totalitarian foes. From the 1960s onward, finally, conservatives have celebrated the one-room school for its rigid discipline and instruction; on the left, meanwhile, partisans praised it as the precursor to group learning, open classrooms, and other pedagogical innovations. Across the political and ideological spectrum, it seemed, everyone envisioned the schoolhouse they needed to see.

Yet politics and ideology cannot, by themselves, account for the enormous grasp the little red schoolhouse has upon the American historical imagination. Nor can we reduce it to the influences of powerful national elites, who are defied—but never deposed—by ordinary local folk.[4] Such perspectives ignore the everyday experiences of America's irreducibly diverse population;

even more, they do not explain how one simple icon can unite these different constituencies into a single, symbolic whole. Across history, to be sure, cultural leaders like Rod Paige have tried to manipulate the little red schoolhouse to serve their present-day political purposes; just as clearly, challengers like Christopher Knight have enlisted the image to advance their own goals. But these machinations cannot help us grasp why a Madison Avenue clothier marketed a "back-to-school" sweater with a one-room red schoolhouse on the front; why a Michigan antique store in a strip mall calls itself Little Red Schoolhouse; why several recent best-selling children's novels take place in one-room schools; or why two episodes of the crass cartoon satire *South Park* featured the song "School Days," the now-classic ode to the single-teacher school.[5] To understand these popular representations, we need to study a much broader swath of social activities—including art, music, fashion, and film—than "politics" can reasonably incorporate. And we need a theory to explain what binds them together into a collective image, retaining enormous sway over all Americans.

Any such theory must start with Americans' deep ambivalence toward progress itself, the idea that humankind in general—and Americans in particular—are steadily improving in knowledge, morality, and happiness. Americans like to think of their nation at the helm of history's positive arc, leading the world into ever-better spheres of conduct and contentment. Yet despite the prevalence of this idea—or, perhaps, because of it—they are also gripped by a profound nostalgia, a yearning for yesterday that has obsessed every generation since the birth of the republic. The faster Americans move forward, indeed, the more they pine for the past; plunging headlong into progress, they fear they are leaving something vital behind. *Nostalgia* derives from the Greek noun *nostos* (return home) and from *algia* (longing). So it literally refers to homesickness, which Renaissance-era physicians described as a physical malady; afflicting soldiers, especially, it was treated with leeches, emetics, and opium. Today we think of nostalgia as a wistful and oftentimes pleasurable emotion, which brings us back to a home that no longer exists—or never did. And the little red schoolhouse is a perfect conduit for this feeling, because it is both a school *and* a house. When Americans imagine it, they are home.[6]

Home, of course, means many things to many people. But most of all it conjures family, the intimate configuration of human beings who create and nurture others. Not surprisingly, then, much of the passion for the little red schoolhouse stems from its symbolic association with familial patterns, habits, and rituals. Observing Minnesota's last one-room school in 2002, a reporter raved about its many "family touches": children's heights were penciled on a doorjamb, they brought their dogs to visit, and everyone went fishing during lunch hour. To others, meanwhile, the little red schoolhouse embodied the stable, close-knit family structure that Americans desired—but rarely sustained. In the 1978 children's novel *To the Tune of a Hickory Stick*, a young girl even takes refuge in the local one-room school to escape her sadistic guardian. "I couldn't ever, never remember being so happy in my whole life before," she notes. "God was surely good to me, getting to live in the schoolhouse with my beloved books, my beloved brother, and my loved, loved teacher." Eventually the teacher marries her mother, who was widowed years before, and everyone lives happily ever after. But in the real world, Americans knew, things were rarely so tidy. "The families are just not close anymore," admitted one New Yorker, restoring an old one-room school in 2004. "It is really different and it's nobody's fault. It just happened—it's progress." Progress was inevitable, in short, but so were its costs.[7]

A second set of costs lay in the realm of "community," another standard focus for schoolhouse nostalgia. Despite its many advantages, the argument goes, modern society has forsaken the neighborly, face-to-face relationships that formerly bound Americans together. And nothing symbolizes this lost community better than the little red schoolhouse, which connected different families into an integrated whole. Inside the classroom, children learned to share and care for one another; and the school itself served as an anchor for the community, a site for evening meetings and a fulcrum of local pride. "We didn't have electricity, no radios, no TVs, poor roads, not many telephones—but we had our schools," recalled a South Dakota woman who taught in the early twentieth century. Since then, it seemed, Americans had gained the whole world of technological conveniences and lost the soul of their communities. "How often have you seen your neighbor lately?" asked one Michigan woman in 1993, bemoaning the demolition of her old one-room school. "Do you play cards together, dance and laugh together, talk over your plans and problems and the state of the nation?" Americans did all of that in the one-room school, of course, but now it was gone. "They say it went to make way for 'progress,' but it hurts," she concluded. Bracketed with quotation marks for good measure, "progress" never quite lived up to its advance billing. Providing material riches, it impoverished Americans in the ways that mattered most.[8]

Last, and somewhat paradoxically, the little red schoolhouse also came to signify the country's lost values of individualism: freedom, hard work, and self-reliance. On the one hand, Americans worried, contemporary society was fraying communal bonds; on the other, it inhibited individual initiative, persistence, and responsibility. But the little red schoolhouse could represent both community *and* individualism, which more than any other factor helps explain its long-standing symbolic power. In the early 1990s, one Michigan citizen praised the one-room school for fostering caring personal relationships—and also for insuring that children took care of themselves. "Those were the days of Rugged Individualism," he wrote, noting that students worked hard in school and then did farm chores when they got home. "We go about ruining our own children by being too good to them." In a preface to the leading history of the one-room school, likewise, former First Lady Barbara Bush described it as a "community center" as well as a beacon of personal improvement. "Despite their real hardships, country schoolchildren . . . learned a curriculum steeped in such values as honesty, industry, sobriety, and patriotism—values we all cherish," Bush wrote. If there were tensions between the community and the individual, they melted away in the happy haze of the little red schoolhouse.[9]

Bush's paean to patriotism points to a final symbolic role for the one-room school: as an emblem of the nation. From the turn of the twentieth century, the little red schoolhouse took its place alongside the flag, eagle, and Uncle Sam in the American patriotic pantheon. Like these other symbols, the one-room school would be invoked by a vast array of citizens for an equally wide array of purposes. Yet after mid-century, when most of the real one-room schools closed their doors, almost nobody questioned the emblem itself. The little red schoolhouse stood for America writ large, so it was an unvarnished good, even when—or especially when—America lost sight of its lessons. "Patriotic songs were learned and sung, the flag salute meant a lot to each pupil, and the picture of Washington was held in respect," wrote a former one-room-school teacher in 1980, lamenting the alleged decline in national pride. By remembering the little red schoolhouse, then, Americans could rediscover their patriotic passion. "I am sure that all of those, who were taught, and learned their A B C's and 3 R's . . . would agree that those one-room, country schools, located within a walking distance of every child, were the Cornerstone, and the Teachers were the Keystones of the Greatest Nation on earth, the United States of America," wrote one memoirist, in a typical passage. He concluded with an unattributed piece of verse, which focused on the ambiguities of memory itself. "You have your memories, and I have mine./Remembrance has brought/Both delight and regret in our time."[10]

This book weaves together personal and collective memories of the one-room school. Inevitably, they shape each other: you have your memories and I have mine, but we are both influenced by the shared stories passed down across the generations. These stories are "true" in a mythological sense but often inaccurate in a historical one, departing from what "really" happened, as best we can determine, in the American one-room school. In the pages that follow, however, I am less interested in exposing these distortions—nobody likes a scold!—than in explaining who remembered what. Across other times and into our own, the little red schoolhouse has brought remembrances of both delight and regret. This book tries to figure out why.

PART ONE

History

In 1897, Clifton W. Johnson wrote an introduction to a new edition of The District School as It Was, by One Who Went to It. Published first in 1833 by Warren Burton, a New Hampshire minister, the book recounted Burton's childhood terrors and triumphs in a one-room schoolhouse. Sixty years later, it remained one of America's most popular historical accounts of its "old" country schools. Like all sources, however, it was incomplete, and as time elapsed, the book had assumed a rosy hue. "We have only fragmentary reminisces left," wrote Johnson, who had written his own history of New England rural schools several years earlier. "We are bringing the old furniture down from the garrets, and setting it forth in the places of honor in our best rooms; and the same feeling that prompts this love for an ancient chair or 'chest of drawers' makes us prize the reminisces of bygone times." Indeed, Burton himself had warned of the same problem when he wrote his book. "The Old

School-house, how distinctly it rises to existence anew before the eye of my mind!" Burton wrote. "As I look back on it, faintly traced on memory, it seems like a beautiful dream."

How do you write the history of a dream? Americans believe deeply in education; since the mid-nineteenth century, moreover, most of them have attended school for at least part of their lives. So when they look back at the institution, the literary scholar Richard Allen Foster observed in 1930, they have a "widespread tendency . . . to surround it with romance." By combining these memoirs with other sources— letters, photographs, newspaper articles, government reports—we can obtain a more balanced, textured picture of the one-room school. The little red schoolhouse was not red, but it was little; it typically had three windows on each side and a single door in front; its children sat on benches and later at individual desks; and so on. Determining what happened inside the building is a much more difficult task. Most teachers were young, female, and single; overseeing a huge array of ages and ability groups, they instructed mainly by rote. Children read and recited from textbooks until they had memorized vast pages of story and rhyme, and those who made trouble were beaten with sticks, one of many schoolhouse punishments that Americans devised. In the evenings, finally, the school hosted dramas, debates, and dances. In many parts of rural America, indeed, the school was often the sole public building and the only center of community life.

To be sure, America's roughly quarter-million one-room schools differed widely from one another. New frontier communities in the North built their first schools from logs; on the prairie, out of sod; and in the

Southwest, from adobe. In wealthier areas, some schools boasted arched windows, columned facades, and other ornamental touches. The quality of instruction varied sharply as well. For every memoir praising the one-room school and the education it provided, a corresponding account describes boredom, frustration, and terror. "Sour old Monday has come and with it school," one weary student wrote in his diary in 1869; the next year, also on a Monday, he inveighed against "School School Forever." But most of these bad memories would be forgotten when the one-room school closed its single door, opening a new entry into sentimentalism and nostalgia. "The historical ghost of the little red school-house stalks the land," wrote the frustrated educational official D. F. R. Rice in 1939, bemoaning a spate of rosy accounts. "It seems a ghost that just cannot be laid. It may have ninety-nine lives." We turn then to the history of the one-room school, mindful of the many spirits that continue to haunt its memory.

ONE

The One-Room Schoolhouse as History

In 1902, at the dawn of a new century, the University of Wisconsin education professor Michael V. O'Shea pleaded for an honest history of the "old-fashioned" one-room school. "For many decades the little red schoolhouse has occupied a coveted place in the affections of the American people," O'Shea acknowledged. Yet its real story was far less impressive than the romance enshrouding it, he added. Four years later, in another appeal for an accurate account of the one-room school, O'Shea pointed out, "There is in the breast of all of us a deep reverence for what our ancestors did, but when an unbiased man, trained in historical method, looks over the past and compares it with the work of today . . . the times past do not seem so glorified."[1]

O'Shea was right. A zealous advocate for school consolidation, O'Shea himself was hardly an "unbiased man" on the history of the little red schoolhouse. But as he correctly perceived, most rural schools never matched the pastoral, sentimental images Americans attached to them. Consider the report filed by a teacher near Scituate, Massachusetts, in 1838. "My name is Eliza B.," the report began. "I am 15½ years old." Boarding in a local home, Eliza B. received $1.25 per week to teach a single seven-and-a-half-week term. That was all she could take. "About the schoolhouse," Eliza B. wrote, "I wish to say the roof is all gone in one corner. You can see outside. The windows are all broken but we put paper over them. The floor is gone right under the bad roof. The fireplace does not heat except right in front of it. The wood was very wet at times as there is no woodshed. There are no conveniences for boys or girls." Children drank from a shared bucket of water, Eliza B. added, but the school was often so cold that the water froze. There was no blackboard, no teacher's desk, and not enough books to keep the school's seventeen students occupied. So they often stayed home, especially in inclement weather, and when they came, they tormented the young teacher. "The big boys took my bell so I could not call them in," Eliza B. wrote. Once inside the schoolhouse, meanwhile, students made a purposely "loud noyse" by scratching their slates. "My uncle brought me here in his slay," she concluded. "I do not care to come back."[2]

To be sure, not all of America's early country schools were as dilapidated or disorganized as this one. Nor did the one-room schoolhouse disappear with the advent of the new century, as

O'Shea so fervently hoped. Whatever its virtues and vices, indeed, the one-room school proved to be one of the most stable, durable institutions in American history. In 1913, on the eve of World War I, fully one-half of the nation's schoolchildren attended one of its 212,000 single-teacher schools. As America urbanized, fewer and fewer children went to one-room schools. But the schools themselves endured, especially in the Midwest and Plains states. In 1936 one-teacher schools made up 71 percent of all schools in Illinois; in Kansas, 72 percent; in Iowa, 77 percent; in Minnesota and Wisconsin, 79 percent; and in South Dakota, 88.5 percent. Only with the advent of World War II and the postwar baby boom did the one-room school truly disappear, transforming rapidly from a living institution into a historical relic. By 1960, just 1 percent of American students went to a single-room school.[3]

Across these long years, meanwhile, the one-room school remained remarkably static in its appearance, layout, and organization. In 1957, when Connecticut's last one-room school closed its doors, its longtime teacher observed that "there ha[d] been little change" since she attended the same school seven decades earlier. Just like her own teacher, Miss Mary J. Kelley still summoned children to school with her "old-fashioned hand-bell." To keep warm in the winter, Kelley's students gathered around an iron pot-bellied stove; to get a drink, they went to the hand-held pump in the front yard; and to answer the call of nature, they visited the two outhouses (his and hers) in the back. "The only modern touch in the school is the telephone," a newspaper reported, "and even that is hidden in a corner."⁴ Compared to Eliza B.'s ramshackle temple of learning, of course, Mary Kelley's school enjoyed many modern conveniences: a blackboard, full sets of textbooks, paned windows, and a roof that did not leak. But Eliza B. would have recognized many other features of the one-room school of 1957, starting with the little handbell that Kelley rang—and that Eliza's own students stole. Neither as rundown as critics claimed nor as bucolic as defenders imagined, America's one-room schoolhouses had enough in common across their long history to imprint themselves indelibly upon the national memory.

Not Red, but Little: Building the One-Room Schoolhouse

For the first two hundred years of European settlement in America, the majority of people who attended school went to a one-room schoolhouse. In 1790 just 5 percent of Americans lived in places with populations greater than twenty-five hundred; by 1830 the fraction had crept up to 9 percent. In nascent towns and cities, Americans created a diverse array of educational enterprises to serve an increasingly polyglot citizenry: pay schools, charity schools, dame schools (taught by a woman in her home), infant schools, and so on. Starting in the 1840s, municipal governments began replacing these institutions with a new bureaucratic system of tax-supported two- and three-storied schools that often served hundreds of children each. Yet the vast bulk of Americans still resided in the countryside, where they evolved their own form of educational governance: the local school district. Scattering from village centers into ever-more remote regions, citizens elected school committees (later known as boards) and raised funds from a mixture of private tuition, property taxes, and state aid. By 1850 a greater percentage of Americans under the age of fifteen attended school than in any other nation on earth. At least three-quarters of these pupils studied in small rural districts, where one-room schools were the norm.[5]

Small-scale governance and high enrollment rates went hand in hand. Most Americans probably associate the nation's nineteenth-century educational boom with so-called common-school reformers like Horace Mann and Henry Barnard, who denounced local districts as cesspits of parsimony and inefficiency. Taking aim at tuition fees, especially, the reformers won state laws that required the districts to provide free schooling to every child. But new evidence suggests that many localities were offering free education well before the common-school movement mandated it. No matter how the schools were financed, meanwhile, rural Americans in the North patronized them at a higher rate than either urban northerners or whites in the South. Citizens were more likely to send their children to school—or to tax themselves for education—in communities where they could influence the process directly, either by voting for a school board or by serving on it themselves. As states swept away property qualifications and other restrictions on white male suffrage, American school enrollment passed that of European countries of similar wealth. But the rise was slower in the urban North, where high rates of transience and immigration inhibited voter participation. It was slower still in the South, thanks to the concentration of power in state legislatures rather than local school districts. The less freedom a district had, especially to tax itself, the fewer children attended school there.[6]

Despite these differences, finally, rural Americans evolved a remarkably uniform style of educational architecture: the one-room schoolhouse. Like their homes, these first schoolhouses were usually made of logs. Inexpensive and simple to build, the so-called pioneer or frontier schools were the ideal medium for a young nation on the move. Indeed, we can mark the westward migration of white people by the log-cabin schools they constructed. After graduating from Harvard in 1755, John Adams taught for three years in a one-room log house fifty miles west of Boston; a half-century later, the seven-year-old Abraham Lincoln walked two miles each way to a log school in Hodgenville, Kentucky; and three decades after that, in the 1830s, James Garfield attended a similar school near his home in Chagrin Falls, Ohio. Log schools were built for convenience, not comfort. Woodsmen stacked unhewn logs and stuffed mud, clay, moss, or straw into the spaces between them; they left a few square holes for windows, which were covered with blankets, animal skins, or greased paper. Sometimes they lined the dirt floors with straw, which kept bare feet warm in the winter but also provided a perfect breeding ground for fleas. Settlers in the old Northwest took refuge in these buildings during Indian raids, pointing their guns through the many holes in the schoolhouse walls. Pioneers often described their log schools as cabin forts or even arsenals, the advanced guard of white civilization against the alleged savagery of Native Americans.[7]

As communities stabilized, they replaced their log schools with frame ones. Here, too, schools provided both a measure and a symbol of frontier development: the more permanent or settled a district, the more likely its school was to be frame instead of log. As early as 1833, just 707 of New York State's 7,685 wood schoolhouses were made of log; in 1871, only 120 log schools remained. Poorer and less populated, the West and South took a bit longer to shift away from log. But the trend, if not the timing, was the same everywhere. By 1907, North Dakota had 3,808 frame schoolhouses and just 30 log ones; 16 others were made of sod, a common nineteenth-century building material on the prairie frontier. Kentucky still had more than 1,000 log schools in 1900. But it also boasted nearly 7,000 frame schools, echoing the national pattern. By 1913, when the United States had more than 200,000 one-room schools, only 5,000 were constructed of log. Whenever a community became large enough, one of Pennsylvania's last one-room teachers recalled, it would replace its "Little Log Schoolhouse" with a "Little Red Schoolhouse."[8]

But most of the time, the schoolhouse was not red. One-room schools were typically white or left unpainted, weathering to silver or gray. "Ours was not the 'little red schoolhouse' we read about," wrote a Boston woman in 1905, looking back on the 1830s village of her youth, "for not one drop of paint ever touched it either inside or out." Some districts did paint their schools in "Venetian red," the inexpensive pigment used in barn paint, which came from iron ore. After the United States developed its own lead supply, however, white paint—derived from lead oxide—became the cheapest option. Even in the rare instances in which a school was built of brick, the mineral content of local clay often rendered it yellow or beige instead of red. School boards argued vehemently over the color of schools: in one rural New York community, advocates of red and white compromised by painting the school in a checkerboard design. Red seems to have been more common in the Northeast, which provided yet another excuse for other regions to eschew it: since red was the color of New England, a Georgia woman declared in 1922, her own state's schools should be white. As early as 1890, when an Ohio poet published a tribute to the "little red schoolhouses" of the Buckeye State, an enterprising reporter found that only 2 of 132 nearby schools were red. (A second journalist mocked the author of the exposé as a "heartless gradgrind," joking that the poem would be "read" even if the schools were not.)[9]

Whatever its color, though, the little red schoolhouse *was* little. Nearly all schools were boxlike squares or rectangles, with sides ranging from 15 to 40 feet. Each of the long sides had three or four tall windows, extending almost from floor to ceiling, without shades or curtains. To keep light out of students' eyes, teachers sometimes put cardboard across the windows; when glass panes broke, a common enough occurrence, they would plug the space with hats or scarves. Schools built after 1900 often had windows on only one side of the building, making it easier for pupils to see. Students entered through a single door, although later schools sometimes included two—one for girls and one for boys—to prevent what an architect called "improprieties between the sexes." The only aesthetic embellishments to this plain structure centered upon the belfry and bell, which enlivened the skylines of the roof and added height to a low building. More than any other feature, two observers wrote in 1899, the bell tower served as the "distinguishing mark" of the one-room school. Resembling nothing so much as a church steeple, the belfry reflected the close link between religion and education in the early republic; for the same reason, post-1900 schools tended to omit it. Other schools built belfries but left them empty, balking at the often prohibitive cost of a church-style bell. Instead, they called children to school with the teacher's handbell.[10]

Once they got inside, students encountered a floor plan that was every bit as simple and predictable as the schools' exterior. Built-in writing desks with backless benches lined three walls of the room; children faced the wall when they wrote and swiveled around to see the teacher, who sat at a desk on a platform along the fourth wall. Smaller children often occupied another set of benches near the center of the room, where a potbellied stove emitted uneven blasts of heat. "Our principal business was to shake and shiver at the beginning of the school," wrote the minister Henry Ward Beecher in 1866, recalling his boyhood, "and to sweat and stew for the rest of the time." Students sitting near the stove were often too warm, falling off to sleep—and off their benches—as temperatures rose. But those at the periphery were too cold, donning mittens and struggling to turn the pages of their textbooks. Miserly school boards were loath to supply the inefficient stoves, which could consume a cord of firewood (128 feet) per week. So they sent boys out to gather it or skimped by burning green wood, which produced more smoke than heat. "This is a beastly day!! Rain and snow and *school!*" wrote one Nebraska teacher in her diary. "The fire won't burn and we are all huddled up in our sweaters and the children are complaining because we are here. I can't really blame them."[11]

Students also grumbled about their benches, which became a major target of nineteenth-century school reformers like Horace Mann. The benches were too high for younger pupils, whose feet dangled precariously near the stove; along the walls, meanwhile, older students strained to negotiate the narrow spaces between their benches and desks. "Large girls can leave their seats only by placing their feet on a level with their hips," one Connecticut educator worried in 1847, "which it is not always best that females should do." After the Civil War, most schools in the North replaced their benches with rows of individual desks. Papering the countryside with advertisements, a burgeoning school-furniture industry promised improved posture, eyesight, and discipline from the new seating plan. Some desks even came with locks, which caused hilarious mishaps. A forgetful New Jersey boy who had left his key at home forced his hand through a hole in his desk to get his pencil. Neither the pencil nor his hand would emerge, so his teacher sent for the local carpenter. Bounding in with his hatchet and saw, the carpenter laughingly suggested that he chop off the boy's hand. But it was no joke to the young pupil, who sobbed until the carpenter cut out a section of the desk to free him.[12]

Advertisers also promoted blackboards and other "apparatus," the nineteenth century's catchall phrase for teaching aids. Appearing first in the 1840s, commercial blackboards grew into one of the biggest school-supply businesses in the country: by 1922 no fewer than 59 companies produced them. In 1869 Vermont's 2,800 schools—almost all one room—together owned only 329 maps, 206 globes, and 118 dictionaries. By the turn of the century, however, most rural districts in the North were probably supplied with all of this equipment. In these same years came a boom in commercial wall decorations. The 1892 adoption of the Pledge of Allegiance set off a flurry of flag purchases in American schools, which had largely eschewed regular patriotic ceremonies before that time. Flag displays often accompanied framed pictures of George Washington, as more and more states required schools to commemorate his birthday. Sixteen northern states also mandated ceremonies in honor of Abraham Lincoln, whose photo became ubiquitous above the Mason-Dixon Line. But he was taboo in the South, where schools were more likely to hang pictures of Robert E. Lee, Stonewall Jackson, or John Calhoun—if they could afford any equipment at all. One Kentuckian recalled that his school's "chalkboard" was simply a black enamel stripe, painted directly onto a wall. Nor did the school possess a single map, flag, or wall picture.[13]

Across the country, finally, America's children adorned one-room schools with their own illicit decorations—what would today be called graffiti. Instead of spray paint, however, they used penknives. "No Egyptian tomb was ever more becarved with hieroglyphics," wrote one educator in 1876, examining his local schoolhouse. "Seats, walls, desks, corners, wherever a notch could be cut or a scratch made, it was faithfully put in." Many of these images were judged "indecent, profane, and libidinous," as a school board member wrote; indeed, a third educator added, some of them "would make heathens blush." One Vermont school district instituted a three-cent fine for every mark made with a knife, but to little avail; when another New England teacher confiscated his students' knives, they used pencils to make grooves and indentations in the soft wood of their desks.

The most common markings were students' names and initials, which often connected them to parents and other relatives who had attended the same school. After a group of six Texas siblings discovered their father's initials in their schoolhouse, they resolved to carve their own initials nearby. All of them succeeded except the youngest brother, who was caught by the teacher. So the boy simply waited for school vacation, when he climbed in through a window and added his initials to the lengthy family inventory.[14]

Another popular locus for graffiti—and a premier focus of educators' anxiety—was the privy, or outhouse, if such a building existed. Before the Civil War, it rarely did. In 1833, for example, less than a third of the 9,000 schools in New York State offered students a privy. Instead, teachers sent boys and girls to different parts of the woods; on the prairie, where it was more difficult to get out of view, schools held separate recesses for each sex. Boys were whipped for "peeking" at the girls, who sometimes stayed home from school to avoid further embarrassment. Later in the century, when schools started to provide dual outhouses—his marked by a sun, hers by a moon—concern turned to the privies themselves. Not surprisingly, most were filthy. A 1913 study of 131 one-room schools in Wisconsin found that school employees or students in just half cleaned the outhouses even once a year. When a privy hole filled up with human waste and Sears Roebuck catalogues (America's first toilet paper) many schools simply dug a new hole and moved the outhouse around it. One

Missouri school found a sow building a nest for her piglets in the outhouse; other privies housed snakes, raccoons, skunks, and possums. Most of all, educators worried, the outhouses transmitted moral filth in the form of obscene penknife drawings. "There the vile creatures go," wrote one school official, "to write and cut and carve what their vile imaginations feed upon."[15]

Teaching and Learning in the One-Room School

The duty of preventing such evil—and of educating America's rural youth—fell upon the one-room-school teacher. During the early nineteenth century, when schools typically held a winter and summer term, they often employed a male teacher for the winter and a female for the summer. The school calendar followed the rhythms of the farm: children were needed at home to plant in the spring and to harvest in the fall. But older boys were more likely to stay on the farm in the summer months, as well. Fearing that a female teacher could not control the "big boys" during their lone winter term, antebellum school districts tried to hire a man (or "master") for that season. For young men, teaching was typically a brief stepping-stone on the way to another career. At least eight American presidents taught in one-room schools during their early adulthoods, usually lasting just a term or two. After a single year at a log-cabin school in South Carolina, Andrew Jackson tired of preparing lessons and decided to read for the law instead; a century later, Warren G. Harding described his brief teaching stint (at a school called White House, ironically) as "the hardest job I ever had." The most accomplished teacher-president was James Garfield, who worked in five schools in the 1850s. Like most male teachers, however, he had higher ambitions. "You and I know that teaching is not the work in which a man can live and grow," Garfield told a friend.[16]

After the Civil War schools shifted to a single term of six to nine months, usually taught by a single female teacher. By 1900 nearly three-quarters of American teachers were women; in one-room schools, the fraction was even higher. In North Dakota, for example, women made up 85 percent of one-room-school teachers in 1916. Most of the teachers were in their teens or young twenties, fewer than 10 percent had any education beyond high school, and virtually all were unmarried; across the country, most districts barred married women from the profession. Like their male counterparts, female teachers changed jobs frequently. Some women moved to get a higher salary, others to get away from a menacing man. In one notorious 1935 episode, a jilted suitor shot a teacher to death in front of her seven students and then took his own life. Exhausted by their responsibilities and repeated job changes, still other women decided to wed in order to escape the classroom: after working in seven schools in nine years, a Texas teacher wrote in her diary, no one could blame her for "marrying to quit." When districts finally relaxed their restrictions on married women, females dominated one-room teaching as never before. By 1958, when the nation's teaching force was still 73 percent female, 92 percent of its one-room instructors were women.[17]

Their duties were enormous. Teachers woke up early to stoke the school stove and also kept it fed during the day, sometimes going outside to gather wood. They swept the floor, patched walls and windows, and painted blackboards. They supervised recess and attended to students' scrapes, falls, and other mishaps. Most of all, they struggled to teach basic literacy and numeracy to a vast array of students—all in the same room, and all at the same time. Some schools in the 1830s and 1840s jammed their narrow benches and desks with a hundred pupils, ranging in age from three to twenty. Later in the century, as rural populations plummeted, schools often faced the opposite problem: too few students. Nearly half of New York State's 8,000 one-room schools in 1915 reported an average attendance of ten students or fewer—including 172 schools with three children, 74 with two, and 13 schools that had exactly one. To be sure, some schools continued to suffer overcrowding. By 1920 the average enrollment in an American one-room school was thirty-one, with one-quarter reporting fifteen students or fewer. So a healthy number of schools exceeded the mean, as well. In Delaware, for example, 39 of 224 one-room schools packed forty or more children between their walls.[18]

Whether out of conviction or necessity, teachers relied almost entirely upon rote methods—that is, memorization—to instruct the diverse ages in their charge. Theoretically, students were grouped according to the level of their primer, or reading book. In the days before free textbooks, however, parents often sent children to school with whatever books they happened to own. So students read one or two books over and over again, periodically moving to the recitation bench near the teacher's desk to regurgitate it back. In the antebellum era, it was not uncommon for a young child to memorize an entire two-hundred- or three-hundred-page text. As localities and states improved their educational funding and the textbook industry centralized, schoolbooks became more standardized. The most popular text was William McGuffey's *Eclectic Reader*, which sold at least fifty million copies; after the King James Bible, "McGuffey" (as it was colloquially known) was probably the most widely read book in America. Published in three editions over the nineteenth century, the book presented a cheery, idealized version of white Protestant life. Poems and stories encouraged patriotic loyalty and individual diligence, warning children about the dangers of idleness and strong drink. "American" habits were, by definition, Protestant ones. By corollary, non-Protestants were something less than American.[19]

Especially on the Great Plains, however, many one-room students were not Protestant; even more, large numbers of them were newcomers to the nation. In 1890, the year after it achieved statehood, North Dakota counted a population of 43 percent foreign born; by 1910 the fraction had swelled to 71 percent. Scandinavians, Germans, and Middle Eastern immigrants swarmed into the state, bringing their own languages and religions; in the tiny town of Ross, for example, Syrian settlers erected America's first mosque. In South Dakota, meanwhile, one teacher found himself with a school of fifty Native American children. Only two of them spoke English. Some teachers tried to accommodate these differences, translating textbooks into non-English languages or even, if the instructor was able, teaching in one. As a young boy in Texas, for example, future president Lyndon Johnson attended a school where much of the instruction took place in German. In most cases, however, teachers fell back on the tried-and-true system of recitation from a shared set of textbooks. Rote methods provided the safest and simplest way to control a wide array ages, ethnicities, and abilities.[20]

But sometimes, rote was not enough; more stringent—and violent—techniques were required. Consider the dilemma of William H. Hamby, who got his first job in the early 1900s at a one-room school in the Ozark Mountains. Unlike most teachers at the time, Hamby had some formal preparation: he had studied at a normal school (teacher-training institution), where his psychology textbook had warned against corporal punishment. But when he was hired, the school board instructed him otherwise. "That's right, make 'em toe the line—lick 'em, lick 'em like the dickens," Hamby was told. And when he reached the classroom, he decided that the school board was right. Teaching eight subjects to fifty-seven pupils, Hamby had to conduct twenty-seven different recitations per day. "And with a class of 15 in the fourth reader and 15 minutes for recitation," Hamby recalled, "how was I to teach Tommy to follow his historical bent in reading, lead Jimmy to love Robert Louis Stevenson, and cultivate Mary in literature, and give Bob the desired start in political research?" Even more, he found, the students in other readers tended to chat, carve their desks, or run around the room instead of reading while the fourth-graders were reciting. So he went outside, pulled ten hickory sprouts from a thicket, and whipped a few of the big boys. After that, the class was quiet—so quiet, Hamby boasted, that he could often hear the tick of his watch.[21]

Not every one-room instructor was as successful in this regard as Hamby. Despite their best efforts, most teachers could not prevent children from whispering or writing notes on their slate boards and passing them along; once sheet paper had replaced slate, students found it even easier to send notes and, worse, launch spitballs. Boys were the most common culprits of schoolhouse mischief, often targeting their female classmates. After schools switched from group benches to individual desks, girls frequently discovered that a boy seated behind them had dipped their braids into the inkwell on his desk. Other favorite forms of bad-boy behavior included climbing the roof and plugging the chimney with branches, which filled the room with smoke; tying the clapper of the school bell to its shell so it would not sound; and throwing buckshot against the blackboard or into the stove, which released loud explosions. After one such episode, a Missouri teacher lined up his male students at the blackboard to search them. The boys stood with their hands behind their backs, passing the buckshot from one to the other; when it reached the last boy, he swallowed it. Privies provided another superb opportunity for mischief. Boys would lock other students inside, tip over the outhouse, or move it in front of the school door.[22]

Like William Hamby, most teachers used corporal punishment, or the threat thereof, to punish such behavior. Minor infractions like talking in class would receive a twist on the ear or a rap on the knuckles from the teacher's ferule, a long, flat ruler that schools kept handy for this purpose. More serious misconduct generated more aggressive floggings, which often assumed a formal or ceremonial tone. Teachers would send the offending student outside to choose a switch; if it was too small or had too many notches, which caused sticks to break, the student would be sent back to select another. Then the student (usually male) would remove his coat or jacket, bend over a chair or table, and receive his punishment. Some offenders tore their pant legs and turned them back underneath, creating a double layer of protection against the master's lash. At least one early Massachusetts school had a whipping post tied to the floor, where all floggings took place; more commonly, students were beaten at the teacher's desk. If two miscreants were at fault, the teacher gave them each a switch and instructed them to strike the other. Just as boys were the most common recipients of corporal punishment, male teachers were more likely to flog than female ones. Exceptions tended to highlight the rule. One Kansas woman beat her sobbing male students with a paddle—known around America as a "board of education"—and then sat down and cried with them, shamed and humiliated by her resort to violence.[23]

Shame and humiliation lay at the heart of other disciplinary measures, which instructors of both sexes employed freely. Teachers rarely put dunce caps on troublemakers, despite the caps' frequent appearance in cartoons and other print media. But schools did develop a wide range of ways to embarrass wrongdoers in the hope of making them do right. Since most miscreants were male—and since the sexes often sat separately in schools— the most common form of degradation was to make a "bad boy" sit with the girls; in some cases, he was also forced to wear a sunbonnet. Other forms of degradation were more closely related to the infraction in question. A student caught chewing gum might be forced to wear it on his nose, head, or ear; a liar would have a split green twig attached to his tongue; and a poor speller was compelled to eat small print letters cut out from a newspaper. As the last example attests, teachers punished students for weak academic work as well as bad behavior. In a common joke from the 1870s, a son asks his father whether a master should "flog a fellow for what he didn't do." The father replies, "Certainly not," and the son quips: "Well, then, he flogged me today when I didn't do my sum!" To nineteenth-century Americans, school failure *proved* naughty conduct. In an era before I.Q. tests and other measures of individual ability, they assumed that slow learners were lazy and inattentive rather than cognitively incapable.[24]

When a schoolmaster became especially violent or sadistic, America's mischievous "bad boys" often joined hands to fight back. After their teacher knocked down one boy with his fist and beat another so badly that he bled, students at a New Hampshire school ripped the ruler from his grasp, hauled him outside, and threw him down an icy hillside. Another New England master had his head thrust into the stove, which singed off his eyebrows; a Virginia teacher was bound hand and foot by his students, who left him in school and went home; Georgia boys followed a drunk instructor into the woods, where they covered him up with branches. Nor could women teachers escape the wrath of bad boys scorned. In the most notorious incident, four boys in Canton, Massachusetts, stoned their feeble teacher to death after she detained them past dismissal time. More commonly, students challenged female teachers with pranks rather than direct physical confrontation. Once women started driving to rural schools, boys pushed their cars into ditches or left dead skunks inside; some female teachers were locked into the outhouse. Finally, teachers of both sexes were routinely barred from the school itself. In a common Christmastime ritual called turning out, boys would come early to school and block the teacher from entry until they received candy. One North Carolina teacher had to pay a half-gallon of brandy, which was gladly consumed by the villagers who had gathered to watch this mock battle unfold.[25]

School and Community

As the final example illustrates, one-room schools provided a central venue for community life in rural America. The first print reference to the term *little red schoolhouse* dates to 1834, when a New Hampshire newspaper published a short story about a town meeting that took place in the school. Often the only public building for miles, one-room schools hosted political rallies, election-day voting stations, and a wide variety of social events: marriages, funerals, picnics, dances, and more. Schools raised money by sponsoring "box socials," where men would bid on elaborately decorated boxes that contained a lunch or dinner. As an added prize, the anonymous female who had prepared the meal would consume it with its purchaser: across rural America male suitors spent considerable time and anguish trying to guess which box their sweetheart had assembled. One-room schools also featured evening dramatic productions and debates, which provided the sole entertainment in many parts of the country. One Utah school staged a debate to ask whether "a load of seed potatoes" or "a load of women" was "most needed in the community"; in North Dakota, local orators deliberated whether "the Farm Woman Works Harder and has Less Recreation than the Farm Man." (A three-judge panel decided in favor of the farm woman.)[26]

But the most common form of evening entertainment came from the pupils themselves, who gave periodic "exhibitions" in the schoolhouse. Nervous parents would gather to watch their children recite speeches from Daniel Webster or Patrick Henry, calculate sums in their heads (a practice known as mental arithmetic), or compete in what H. L. Mencken would later call a "peculiarly American institution": the spelling bee. This competition was known initially as a spelldown because children who erred had to take their seats, or simply as a spelling school, in which students moved to the front or the back of the class. Satirists like Mencken and Mark Twain enjoyed heaping vitriol on the spelling bee, which required children to memorize and regurgitate hundreds of obscure words. But the children themselves seemed to delight in the practice, precisely because it lent interest to an otherwise tiresome subject. "The child cares no more in his heart about the arrangement of vowels and consonants in the orthography of words, than he does how many chips lie one above the other at the schoolhouse woodpile," wrote an observer in 1833, in one of the earliest recorded descriptions of a spelling bee. "But he does care whether he is at the head or foot of his class." Others remarked that girls possessed a special affinity for spelling bees, because they supposedly cared more for visual appearance—in words, as in clothes—than boys did. Still others claimed that immigrant children excelled in the competition, which echoed the rote pedagogy of their homelands; even more, spelling bees let anyone who worked hard, regardless of background, rise to the top.[27]

Schools also provided a natural location for a wide variety of community holidays and celebrations: Valentine's Day, Mother's Day, Arbor Day, and more. After the Civil War, veterans of the conflict convened at the schoolhouse on Memorial Day; starting in the 1880s, they often presented the school with a flag. The biggest social event of the year occurred near Christmas, when the community gathered in the school to sing, pray, and watch students stage a play or pageant. Shepherds, wise men, and the baby Jesus mingled easily with fairy godmothers, ghosts, and elves. The most exciting moment was the arrival of Santa Claus, who bounded merrily into the school and deposited presents under the tree. Sometimes he would be preceded by his "reindeer," men wearing elk or deer antlers. Schools in the pre-electricity era lit their Christmas trees with candles, which presented an obvious safety hazard. At one Michigan school, even Santa Claus's beard caught on fire. "Santa rushed outside, followed by two or three other men," one young witness recalled. "When they returned I didn't see Santa, but I did see a man with clothes like the ones Santa had been wearing."[28]

One-room schoolhouses also hosted more formal religious worship, especially in remote areas that lacked a church. In many communities, indeed, the school and church buildings were one and the same. School bells rang out on Sundays to welcome worshipers for prayer; often, the teacher would also conduct Sunday School for the same children she educated during the week. In places with a church but no school, students would meet in the house of worship for their daily schoolhouse instruction. Where both institutions existed, they reinforced each other. One-room schools echoed churches not just in their bell-tower architecture but also in their religious names: Jerusalem, Zion, Paradise Chapel, or sometimes simply "Church." Most of all, the public school taught a generic Protestantism as part of its regular, state-sanctioned curriculum. Teachers began each day with a prayer and a reading from the Bible; students memorized long passages of Scripture, reciting them back at evening exhibitions; and schools would open their doors to periodic revivals and traveling evangelists like "Uncle Glen Perry," who thrilled Michigan children in the early twentieth century with Bible stories and puppet shows. Religious dissent was rare. As a teacher from upstate New York recalled, anyone who did not wish to participate simply kept silent.[29]

But not always. Consider Daniel Freeman, known as "America's first homesteader," who brought his large family to Nebraska in 1871 and built a schoolhouse of handmade brick. Nearly thirty years later, Freeman objected to Bible exercises conducted by the new teacher at the school. Arguing that her teaching violated Nebraska's ban on "sectarian" instruction in public schools, Freeman took the case to district court, where he was rebuffed. So he appealed to the Nebraska Supreme Court, which ruled in Freeman's favor in 1902. But the court stressed that the Bible was not a sectarian book, in and of itself; the problem lay only in the teacher's sectarian *interpretation* of Scripture, the court said, which *could* be read "without comment." After that, Freeman presented himself regularly at the school to listen to the Bible—and ensure that the teacher did not embellish it. In most places dissenters were neither as zealous nor as bold as Daniel Freeman. So sectarian instruction persisted well into the 1950s and 1960s, despite clear state and federal court injunctions against it. Warned that her daily prayer ceremonies might violate state law, one Texas teacher simply continued the practice—and kept her job. So did Protestant teachers in heavily Catholic schools, where parents objected to readings from the King James Bible.[30]

In districts that were entirely Catholic, on the other hand, schools used the Douay or Catholic Bible; frequently, they also taught in non-English tongues. But populations in mixed communities clashed bitterly over religion, and especially over language, belying the happy images of harmony that pervade so many present-day depictions of the one-room schoolhouse. In North Dakota, where three-quarters of the students were first- or second-generation immigrants, one native-born teacher threatened to whip a newcomer from Norway for failing to pronounce *j* and *y* in the proper manner; another teacher condemned her Icelandic female students for their "indecent" tradition of retaining family names after marriage; still others banned foreign languages during recess, assessing fines and floggings for those who refused to comply. To be sure, some instructors showed sympathy and sensitivity toward cultural differences. One teacher translated her entire first-grade reader into Icelandic, then repeated each lesson in English; several others staged "A Program of All Nations" at their schoolhouse to highlight students' handiwork, costumes, and folk dances. "Let the night belong to the foreign patrons," two North Dakota teachers urged. "Show your appreciation of their efforts. . . . Be sincere in this." For the most part, however, native-born teachers treated their "foreign" students with open disdain. "The dutch got my opinion of them, *they know nothing*," underlined one Wisconsin school official, using the derogatory term for Germans. "The German language, catechism, and parental interference seem to be an insufferable barrier," complained another.[31]

As the final remark suggests, immigrant parents often presented themselves at the schoolhouse to protest. Some condemned teachers' religious proselytizing; others demanded instruction in their own tongues, lest their children continue to suffer in bewilderment and shame. Teachers referred confused immigrant students to the English dictionary, parents complained, which baffled them even further with "a maze of words that had no meaning." Some children managed to memorize their lessons, but could not comprehend what they were reciting; others simply sank into their seats, as one immigrant novelist recalled, hoping the teacher would ignore them. Behind the scenes, meanwhile, immigrant parents worked to replace so-called American teachers with members of their own ethnicity. Most native-born teachers came from some distance, so they needed to board with local families, but some communities could not find a single household to take in their new instructor, which forced county authorities to hire "untrained local people"—immigrants—for the school. In remote Mountrail County, North Dakota, one Norwegian Lutheran pastor agreed to board a young teacher. But when he learned she could not speak Norwegian, he rescinded the offer.[32]

The frequent practice of boarding teachers from outside the district further complicates the consensual, communal image of the one-room school. Charged with keeping order in the school and keeping parents happy, new teachers often found that they could not do both. On the issue of discipline, indeed, many communities were deeply divided. Some parents encouraged the teacher to beat their children, promising to beat them again at home if they acted up in school. As a token of his support, one Kentucky father even presented the new instructor with a paddle. Like schoolboys, however, other parents challenged teachers whom they saw as too cruel or brutal. In the face of an overly violent master, in fact, some parents responded with violence of their own. One angry Missouri father went to school and drew a knife on the teacher, who drew his own blade, and invited the teacher to a duel; in Illinois, several parents tried to seize a sadistic master and scuffled with school board members who sought to protect him. After his mother whipped an insolent girl at the school where she taught, the future historian Thomas Clark watched warily as the girl's father galloped toward his house, but instead of challenging Clark's mother, the man dismounted from his horse and thanked her. Clark and his mother let out sighs of relief, temporarily released from the tension that often surrounded school discipline.[33]

Other common sources of community friction included the site of the school and, not surprisingly, the taxes to pay for it. Penny-pinching boards often erected schools on the cheapest possible land, which few others wanted. Preferred locales included the eroded patches at the top or bottom of a hill, low-lying swamps, and the irregular triangles created by the intersection of roads, fields, and railroad tracks. One-room buildings were sometimes so close to wheel tracks that schools placed a large stone or boulder in front of their exposed edge, to protect it from passing vehicles. As might be expected, wealthier citizens exerted a disproportionate influence upon the site selection. Some large estate holders wanted the school near their property or even on it, donating the land for the building to ensure that it remained close to home. Others tried to prevent schools from locating nearby, fearful that youngsters would trample their crops or vandalize their fences. Debates over sites often split communities, continuing well after a school was built. Lawrence, Kansas, erected its first one-room school on the town's east side; late one night, a group of westsiders hitched their horses to the school and dragged it to their neighborhood, and a few evenings later, the eastsiders "stole" it back. Around the country, students arriving for school were often surprised—and delighted—to discover that it had been moved elsewhere.[34]

Most of all, communities bickered over who should pay for the schools—and how much. One of Mark Twain's earliest memories from his hometown of Hannibal, Missouri, involved a contentious town meeting, where frugal taxpayers proposed to shut down the local school. "It's not a real saving," one farmer countered, "for every time you stop a school you will have to build a jail." His argument echoed common-school reformers like Horace Mann and Henry Barnard, who pleaded with citizens, often in vain, to invest in education. "The rich man who has no children declares that the exaction of a contribution from him to educate the children of his neighbor is an invasion of his rights of property," Mann wrote. "The man who has reared and educated a family of children denounces it as a double tax when he is called upon to assist in educating the children of others also; or, if he has reared his own children without educating them, he thinks it peculiarly oppressive to be obliged to do for others what he refrained from doing even for himself." A Connecticut teacher voiced similar complaints that same year in a letter to Barnard, author of the nation's most famous exposé of the American schoolhouse. Denouncing everything from backless benches to putrid privies, Barnard's *School Architecture* had been sent to each town in eight states by 1855; all told, 125,000 copies of the book circulated nationwide. Yet most local taxpayers remained satisfied with the status quo, as the teacher told Barnard. "The schools and schoolhouses of this town are in the poorest order," he wrote, "but little or no exertion is made by the citizens to make them better." Only in the twentieth century would one-room schools undergo widespread improvements—right before they began to melt away.[35]

Twentieth-Century Schoolhouses and the Burden of Race

Two major trends marked one-room schools in the United States after 1900. The first was a steady improvement in schoolhouse conditions and, probably, in the education that rural children received. The biggest burst of reform took place during the Progressive era, when a characteristic blend of voluntary and state action made single-teacher schools brighter, cleaner, and more pleasant places to learn. Especially in the South, female civic groups raised money and offered prizes for schools whose patrons added fresh coats of paint, planted gardens, purchased maps, or placed pictures on the walls. Drawing upon well-worn gender images, one North Carolina woman resolved to turn ugly school *houses* into attractive "school *homes*." Around the country, meanwhile, state education officials distributed cardboard "model school houses" and architectural blueprints to local districts; they also circulated "Rural Standardization" scorecards, which allowed communities to rank their school based on its desks, blackboards, and outhouses as well as its average attendance, teacher qualifications, and length of school term. By the 1920s, many of these standards became encoded in state law. New Jersey required that light enter the schoolhouse from the left, to prevent the "cross-lighting" that strained young eyes; Virginia mandated that schools provide at least two "suitable and convenient" outhouses, kept in "a clean and wholesome condition"; and New York specified minimum amounts of floor and air space per child.[36]

The other major twentieth-century trend was rural school consolidation. By 1925 nineteen states had passed laws to encourage one-room schools to merge into larger ones. Minnesota offered school districts $750, $1,000, and $1,500 for each two-, three-, or four-room building they erected; Pennsylvania paid districts $200 for every one-room school they closed. Other states allowed districts to consolidate upon a majority vote in the entire affected area, so that a single district could not exert veto power over the process. Between 1918 and 1928, Americans abandoned one-room schools at the rate of four thousand per year; during the same period, seventeen states closed more than a quarter of their schools. At the simplest level, this trend echoed broad demographic changes: as more Americans moved from smaller communities to larger ones, their schools grew as well. But consolidation also reflected the widening wealth gap between rural and urban America, which opponents of the one-room school exploited to the hilt. "It is a far cry from the little red schoolhouse [with] its small windows, its plain hard benches, and its red-hot stove, to the large palatial structures which are to be

seen in nearly all our cities and growing towns," wrote two educators in a typical passage. Others cited studies showing that
rural children attended school less often than their urban counterparts, suffered more health problems, and so on. "A double
standard of quality for rural and urban educational products is
un-democratic and un-American," one journal editorialized.[37]

Consolidation proponents married this egalitarian rhetoric to
the language of rights, another favorite Progressive-era theme.
"The country child has rights," one educator declared. "He is
entitled to a square deal in opportunities to enjoy the best that
the civilization of the world thus far has produced." According to
a well-worn North Dakota joke, a country school was a building
erected to deprive a child of an education; in a more ominous
vein, one Missourian suggested that rural Americans might become a "menace to the state" if their schools were not enlarged
and improved. But school consolidation could never have occurred without another important state initiative: new road
construction. Students who formerly walked to their one-room
school needed passable roads and a school wagon or bus, the era's
other key innovation, in order to attend a larger, more distant
school. Especially in the South, many state governments invested heavily in roads and buses; others passed laws requiring
districts to provide transportation for children who lived a given
distance from school. Even if a consolidated school was near
enough to walk to, a Georgia educator added, parents would not

let children go there on foot. "Long trips alone would be dangerous," he warned, "in localities infested by roving negroes."[38]

As the final comment suggests, race represented the crucial
limit on twentieth-century rural school reform. African American children were more likely than whites to attend a dilapidated, unimproved one-room school; by the same token, fewer
blacks went to a consolidated one. In the segregated South, black
children could not ride on whites-only school buses; nor did
states provide African Americans with transportation of their
own. So most blacks had little choice but to walk—sometimes as
far as twelve miles a day round-trip—to the nearest one-room
school, which was often little more than a shack. "Many of these
houses are not fit for animals," a black newspaper in Georgia editorialized in 1914. "Cows, horses, and pigs should have better
shelter than are furnished the Negro children in the country."
Even more, the paper added, 75 or 80 black children were sometimes crowded "like a parcel of sheep" into these hovels. Worse,
white children spit or threw objects from their bus windows at
black students who were walking to school. Greene County,
Georgia, expended $36 on each white student and $3 on each
black one, a ratio of 12 to 1; in Macon County, the ratio was 18 to
1. Together, the two counties spent more simply to transport 510
white children to consolidated schools than they spent on the
education of their 5,000 black students, most of whom remained
in one-room schools.[39]

But not all did. African Americans across the rural South built new, larger schools with the aid of the philanthropist Julius Rosenwald, whose fund donated more than $4 million for five thousand black schools between 1917 and 1932. By the end of this period, one in every five African American schools in the South was a "Rosenwald school." From the start, Rosenwald made no secret about his preference for consolidated buildings. "Get away as much as possible from the one-teacher school in favor of two or more teacher school," he wrote in a 1917 memo, marked "Important" by an aide. By 1921 just one-third of the schools he aided were single teacher; and by 1930, when the fund phased out aid to one-room schools altogether, the average Rosenwald school had more than three instructors. To make sure black children could reach these schools, the fund also helped bankroll "Rosenwald buses." The new black buildings were the envy of white citizens, who in turn built their own new schools—and often borrowed Rosenwald blueprints—lest they fall behind African Americans. "The 'white picture' is a very dark one, (so far as the school is concerned)," wrote a white Georgia teacher in 1934. "Let's see if the 'darker ones' can throw a little light our way."[40]

Even after this flurry of construction, however, most black students still attended unimproved, one-room schools. In 1931, when 36 percent of white schools in Alabama had a single teacher, 72 percent of black schools did. The skew was even greater in Georgia, where one-room buildings made up 69 percent of black schools in 1937 but just 19 percent of white ones. Black one-room schools remained as dreary and dilapidated as ever; indeed, they often resembled white log-cabin schools of the previous century. Walls lacked paint or plaster, roofs lacked ceilings, windows lacked panes, and students lacked complete sets of textbooks, reading whatever stray books they could find. "We have in this 'Dark Belt' of Maryland, quite 200 children of free school age, and not a sign of a Rosenwald School," wrote a black minister in a 1934 appeal for funds. "Five schools in name—not fit for children, nor Teachers. But all schools of the other Race are modern. . . .We weep! We cry! We appeal to the authorities, but no attention is paid us." As late as 1959 the baseball hero Jackie Robinson devoted his newspaper column to "the plight of Negro school children" in the rural South. Many were still relegated to "rundown, unsanitary shacks" with just one room.[41]

Similar problems afflicted Mexican Americans in the rural Southwest, where upward of eighty children crowded into dilapidated, segregated one-room schools. Educational officials in this region employed a somewhat different rationale for racial segregation, arguing that Spanish-speaking students needed separate schools in order to attain proficiency in English. But the outcome, too often, was the same: pitiful facilities and poor instruction. The one-room schoolhouse for Mexican Americans in Pecos, Texas—named, ironically, "Union y Progresso"—opened its doors for just sixty days a year, and students squeezed onto backless benches, just as white children had done in the log-cabin era. Most teachers barred Mexican children from speaking Spanish, even during recess, which generated further resentment and confusion. In rural Pima County, Arizona, where a state law mandated English for all instruction, one sympathetic white teacher risked dismissal by allowing her students to put on their annual Christmas play in Spanish. But other Anglos in Pima questioned whether Mexicans needed much formal education at all, given their likely future as manual laborers. "Teach them to read and write a little . . . then leave them alone," one local banker told the teacher. "Somebody has got to do their work, and they like it."[42]

By the 1950s, only 1 percent of children in the United States went to a single-teacher school. But the one-room school played an increased role in America's historical memory, looming ever larger as the actual institution faded away. For obvious reasons, blacks and Mexican Americans rarely indulged in this brand of nostalgia: they had suffered too much from the one-room school to romanticize it. That task was left to white people, who began to praise the virtues of the Little Red Schoolhouse—and to paper over its vices—in the immediate wake of the Civil War. We turn now to the images they created, which changed over time and, inevitably, diverged from the little red schoolhouse itself.

PART TWO

Memory

In 2004, Richard Peck published a jocular children's novel with the evocative title The Teacher's Funeral: A Comedy in Three Parts. The story starts with the death of the hated Miss Myrt, who had ruled the local one-room school with an iron hand. Yet before her day, the preacher declares at her funeral, times were even tougher. "Yes, sisters and brothers, the old schoolhouse, the first schoolhouse—the log schoolhouse with its stick chimbley daubed with clay," he reminisces. "Who remembers when children were happy to learn? Who remembers when children were eager to learn?" The preacher pounds his fist on the pulpit, and one worshiper jumps to her feet: "Tell it like it was!"

Only, it wasn't. As explained by our narrator, a boy named Russell, the preacher "got them to miss the good old days when the winters were worse and the kids were better." And everyone missed the good old days, Russell adds, especially when one-room schools were involved. "It was *only about a mile, and uphill both ways, as the road to school always was back then," he quips, recalling his daily walk to school. "And we were barefoot, as we were all winter in our memories later."*

By satirizing these rosy memories, Peck's story reminds us how profoundly they have influenced Americans' perceptions of the one-room school. Starting in the 1870s, American artists and authors spun a steady halo of nostalgia around the Little Red Schoolhouse. Here they ran afoul of educational leaders and other Progressive reformers, who took aim at one-room schools and the sentimentalism surrounding them: the more Americans romanticized the little red schoolhouse, reformers said, the longer these inadequate single-teacher schools would continue to mar American education. During the Great Depression, likewise, New Deal photographers and other activists condemned one-room schools as cesspools of poverty and inequality. Yet after mid-century, when almost all these schools had passed into history, Americans forged a new unity around their memory. Suddenly everyone loved the little red schoolhouse, albeit for different reasons. To Cold Warriors, the one-room school was a bastion of American democracy, to liberals in the 1960s it was the foremother of cooperative learning and community control, and to the new right of the 1970s and 1980s it was a lodestar of discipline and back-to-basics instruction. The only thing that drew them together was the little red schoolhouse, a sacred symbol of education itself.

So in Americans' memories, the little red schoolhouse will always be good. They might have to walk barefoot in the snow, uphill both ways, but it will be worth it. The schoolmarm will greet them at the door, bell in hand; they will warm their hands at the stove, then take their seats at their desks. They will memorize poems, compete in spelling bees, and compute sums in their heads; they will flirt and giggle and play pranks on the teacher, who will punish them—firmly but fairly—with lashes from a switch. (They deserved it, after all.) Then they will go home to tell the stories all over again, to their parents and siblings and later to their children and grandchildren. "We shape our buildings," Winston Churchill once observed, "and thereafter they shape us." And they continue to do so, long after the buildings themselves are gone, in the ways that we choose to remember them. Only a few hundred one-room schools continue to operate in the United States, while a handful of others have been restored for tourists. But the memory of the little red schoolhouse is all around, influencing Americans' views of the world—and vice versa. We shape our memories, like our buildings, and thereafter they shape us.

Sentiment and Its Critics

In November 1892 a Nebraska newspaper launched a bitter attack upon a popular symbol. It was election season, and candidates of every stripe had seized upon the image of the little red
schoolhouse. Yet according to the *Omaha World-Herald*, country
schools in Nebraska had never resembled the pretty, bright building on campaign posters and buttons; they were dirty, damp, and
cramped. "'The little red school house' so fondly alluded to
sounds very sweet when juggled about in a great collection of sentiment," the *World-Herald* declared, "but the facts are against it."
Better to recognize the newly consolidated schools in the countryside and the "great monuments of education" in the city, the
paper continued, where actual improvement was taking place.
"This city wants real progress and not red paint," the *World-Herald*
concluded. "It wants science and not sentiment."[1]

The paper was alluding to the remarkable celebration of the little red schoolhouse in the American cultural imagination that had begun shortly after the Civil War, when a rapidly urbanizing America started to glorify the one-room school in verse, song, and art. The trend picked up steam during the so-called "patriotic cult" of the 1890s, which made the simple, small-town little red schoolhouse into a symbol of national unity and power. But this surge of sentimentalism would come under fire at the turn of the century from journalists, academicians, state education officials, and other Progressive reformers. For the next thirty years, these mostly urban elites would wage zealous battle against the rural one-room school and its idealized image, the little red schoolhouse. To the Progressives, the two battles were closely related: so long as Americans clung to romantic and distorted conceptions of the past, they would never create a better future. "The chief obstacle that stands in the way is the sentiment for 'the little red schoolhouse,'" wrote one advocate for consolidated rural schools in 1903, punctuating his skepticism with quotation marks.[2]

In many ways, ironically, this excessive sentimentality was the Progressives' own doing. Beneath a host of Progressive initiatives—including child labor laws, playgrounds, and consolidated schools themselves—lay an idyllic image of rural life, which reformers hoped to protect and update for a modern age. By combining decrepit single-teacher schools into larger, better-equipped ones, Progressives said, they would stem the dangerous flow of young people to the city; even more, they would restore the vitality, strength, and simplicity of the countryside. In the urban campaign for multiservice "social centers," likewise, Progressives drew upon a romantic vision of rural life and, most of all, of rural schools. "Nothing in our national life has done so much to foster the spirit of democracy, of spontaneous community thought and sense of solidarity, as this free association of citizens . . . in the schoolhouse in the early days," wrote Rochester's Edward J. Ward, a leading advocate for social centers. The "real ancestor" of the urban social center, Ward added, was "the little red schoolhouse back home."[3]

"Back home" in the real rural community, however, Americans wanted to retain their one-room schools. They invoked classic themes of liberty and self-rule, comparing their campaign to the War of Independence and their foes to King George. But they also summoned bucolic images of the little red schoolhouse that could appeal to city and country folk alike. As millions of Americans left the farm for the metropolis, nothing pulled on their heartstrings more than sentimental poems, pictures, and songs about the red schoolhouse on the hill. In many ways, then, the battle over the one-room school became a struggle over sentiment itself. "The Little Red School House has been part of the very vitals of American institutions," declared rural New Yorker Walter S. Gedney in 1928, "and should it pass with many other things forever into oblivion . . . just so much strength will be taken from our body politic." Responding to charges that he was "too sentimental," Gedney pleaded guilty; indeed, he welcomed "sentimental expressions" on the subject.[4] His remarks appeared in a new rural journal with an old-fashioned title: *The Little Red Schoolhouse.* Only with the disappearance of the one-room school would this image become a true national icon, unmoored from its beleaguered history and beloved by all.

Sentiment, Part 1: Lost Lives and Loves

In March 1870 the physician and author Oliver Wendell Holmes, Sr., wrote a brief, friendly letter to his fellow New England poet John Greenleaf Whittier. The subject was Whittier's new poem "In School Days," which began:

> Still sits the school-house by the road,
> A ragged beggar sleeping;
> Around it still the sumachs grow,
> And blackberry-vines are creeping.

Born two years apart in the first decade of the nineteenth century, Holmes and Whittier had both attended one-room schools. As Holmes savored the poem, his memories came flooding back. "I had no sooner read it than I fell into such ecstasy that I could hardly find words too high-colored," wrote Holmes, father of the famous jurist. "My eyes fill with tears. . . . Many noble, many lovely verses you have written; none that go to the heart more surely and sweetly as these."[5]

For the next half-century, readers across America would commit Whittier's poem to their own hearts. Schoolchildren recited it at assemblies; politicians quoted it at rallies; cartoonists spoofed it in print. "In School Days" marked the beginning of a massive groundswell of sentimentality surrounding rural childhood—including rural schools—after the Civil War. Significantly, "In School Days" first appeared in a children's magazine; in a letter introducing it, Whittier wondered whether it might not be "child*ish*, if not child*like*" and "too spooney for a grave Quaker like myself." He need not have worried. From poets and novelists to vaudevillians and filmmakers, Americans would continue to celebrate the single-teacher school in the same romantic idiom that Whittier invoked. But they would simultaneously bemoan its alleged decline, adding a note of melancholy to the cult of the little red schoolhouse. A decade after he wrote "In School Days," indeed, Whittier visited the one-room school that inspired it and discovered that the school was gone. All that remained were a few foundation stones along with the blackberry vines and sumac, which Whittier gathered in a handful for display in his home. Leaving its messy history by the side of the road, the "ragged beggar" now entered the florid halls of memory.[6]

During the antebellum era, to be sure, handfuls of artists and writers had already begun to romanticize the one-room schoolhouse. In *The Old School House* (1849), for example, the Hudson

River painter James MacDougal Hart depicted a rustic but charming one-room school amid the characteristic grandeur of an upstate New York landscape. A more common—and less comforting—image appeared in Francis W. Edmonds's *The New Scholar* (1845), which showed a schoolboy cowering before a whip-wielding master. Likewise, poets and novelists portrayed the one-room schoolhouse as a place of chaos and violence, not peace and good cheer. In Royall Tyler's *The Algerian Captive* (1797), a teacher strikes an insolent boy only to be threatened by the student's father; in "Death in the School Room (A FACT)" (1841), Walt Whitman's first published story, a brutal master flogs a sleeping boy until he is dead; in the Daniel Pierce Thompson novel *Locke Amsden; or, The Schoolmaster: A Tale* (1847), a kindly instructor wonders why a society that had banned the lash for adults retained it in the one-room school. And in *The Legend of Sleepy Hollow* (1820), Washington Irving gave America one of its best-known antiheroes, Ichabod Crane. His very name, derived from the book of Samuel, suggests degeneracy: "And she named him Ichabod, saying, the Glory is departed from Israel." Tyrannical toward students and ingratiating with the ladies, Ichabod is run out of town by a clever woodsman—with a major assist from a headless horseman.[7]

When antebellum writers referred specifically to the little red schoolhouse, meanwhile, they more often expressed spite than sentimentality. The first print use of the phrase was neutral, alluding to an 1834 town meeting. The next reference occurs nine years later in the student-run *Yale Literary Magazine*, which published a scathing story about a small town. "The village also contained a little red school-house, situated as schoolhouses usually are, in the worst possible place that could be found," the story noted. "There [children] were accustomed daily to congregate, trembling with awe at the birchen sceptre, that was wielded over their heads, and from its shabby portals, not unfrequently would the ears of the passer-by be saluted by shrill and heart-piercing ululations [from] some aspiring but offending genius." Only an 1858 poem in the *Knickerbocker*, a New York literary monthly, suggested any trace of the romance that would soon surround the term. The poet visits the "sweet little hamlet" of his youth, gazing at the "rustic old farm-house" and "the little red school-house." Then he starts to cry, recalling "the frolicksome days I there spent / With the sweet dew of youth on my brow."[8]

Such statements would become commonplace after the Civil War, when the chaos and dislocations of the war, and the swift urbanization that followed it, fueled nostalgia for a simpler time. "Many a boy, after years of absence from his native hills looks back to the little red schoolhouse at the forks of the road, and recalls the days of his tutelage therein, with a degree almost of reverence," declared one Boston newspaper in 1873. No matter that most native-born Americans in Boston had lived in the city since birth, or that most newcomers came from other countries; the sentimental boom made all Bostonians "remember" the little red schoolhouse, even if none of them had ever attended one. The key engine of this process was probably poetry, which middle-class Americans consumed and recited to a degree unimaginable today. Whittier's "In School Days" followed a trope that had already been popularized by the poet and painter Peter Fishe Reed in "The Old School-House" (1868): an older man returns to the now-decrepit little red schoolhouse, recalling the laughs and loves of his youth. Reed's male protagonist botched a word on purpose to let his sweetheart pass him in the spelling bee; in the Whittier poem, the girl apologized for passing the boy. She went to an early grave, but the boy—now a "gray-haired man"—can still recall her "sweet child face."[9]

Widely reprinted in newspapers and school textbooks, "In School Days" spawned hundreds of imitators. Some poets borrowed lines almost directly from Whittier, as in this verse from Troy, New York:

> The little red schoolhouse, alone and forlorn,
> Of all its fair freshness and beauty quite shorn,
> Still sits at the turn of the road.
> The hollyhocks blossom along near the wall,
> And the sunflowers, stately, majestic, and tall,
> Still cheerfully bear up their load.

Others adopted the same general format—longing for the bygone school and a lost love—but added an emphasis on naughty behavior. Consider "The Old Schoolhouse," a 1902 poem by T. S. Denison. The poem begins in classic fashion with a rustic school on a hill but soon moves to a different subject: spitballs. "We chewed our books for paper balls," Denison wrote,

> And slyly tossed them up on high,
> Upon the ceiling, there to dry.
> But well we learned that simple rule:
> "The rod is made for the back of a fool."

Or consider this verse, from an unknown scribe in Missouri:

> Still sits the schoolhouse by the road
> Close by the old oak tree,
> Where many a boy has took a dose
> Of grim old hickory tea.[10]

Here and elsewhere, poets happily recounted their schoolhouse punishments as well as their pranks. To early-nineteenth-century authors like Irving and Whitman, the master's rod embodied pure evil: in the last line of his story about the wicked teacher, Whitman states simply, "Death was in the school-room, and [he] had been flogging a CORPSE." But postbellum writers added a strong dose of romance to the battle between master and student, which came to symbolize the liberty and vitality of a long-lost rural America. In an era of hothouse industrialization and urbanization, indeed, the rural "bad boy" was actually good. By snubbing figures of authority, he quelled fears of "overcivilization"—and thus over-feminization—and reconnected the nation to its founding bedrock of strength, independence, and self-reliance. "Of course all boys are not full of tricks," declared George W. Peck, author of *Peck's Bad Boy and His Pa* (1883), "but the best of them are."[11]

No one was a better target for tricks than the teacher. Consider Mark Twain's first boy hero, Tom Sawyer (1876), who is flogged so often that he says he has a second name—Thomas—for when he is being whipped. ("I'm Tom when I'm good," he adds.) The master's beatings grow more severe as the end-of-year exhibition approaches because he wants the students to make a "good showing" before the parents and school board. But Tom gets the last laugh, lowering a cat by a string to snatch off the teacher's wig during the exhibition. "The boys were avenged," Twain concludes. "Vacation had come." A similarly jovial spirit marks *A Boy's Town* (1902), William Dean Howells's contribution to the bad-boy genre. Although Howells's protagonist lives in fear of his brutal teacher, he also confesses a certain fondness for the man. The master was simply doing his job, Howells writes, just as the boys were doing theirs: to exert their natural exuberance against the dull grind of civilization. By the late 1800s, of course, most American teachers were female. Reflecting back on their own antebellum youths, however, authors like Twain and Howells invariably depicted the teacher, like the bad boy himself, as male. The only way to assert your masculinity, it seemed, was to win a schoolhouse battle with a man.[12]

In *The Hoosier School-Master* (1871), meanwhile, Edward Eggleston narrated this struggle from the point of view of a young teacher. Ralph Hartsook faces a mutiny when the big boys of Flat Creek, Indiana, block him from entering the school, a common student prank. So Hartsook borrows a second schoolboy trick: pouring gunpowder down the chimney. The boys emerge shaking from the explosion and wiping smoke from their eyes. Hartsook also subdues the school bully by suggesting that they join an imaginary "Church of the Best Licks," which creates a rough parity between them. (In his preface, Eggleston underscored the significance of this earthy metaphor: although the book was not based on his own life, he "should like to be considered a member of the Church of the Best Licks.") Starting as a three-part magazine series, *The Hoosier School-Master* caused such a stir that Eggleston quickly added thirteen more installments and released a book version; shortly thereafter, it appeared in French (as *Le maitre d'école de Flat Creek*) and in German. Readers thrilled to its theme of masculine rivalry—good teacher versus bad boys—as well as its portrayal of a spelling bee, a common antebellum practice that had lost popularity. After his book became a best seller, Eggleston boasted, schools as far away as Australia revived the old-time spelldown.[13]

Eggleston's book was illustrated by the prominent cartoonist Frank Beard, but Beard's drawings, like most book art of the period, were in black and white. Coloring the school would be left to painters like Winslow Homer, whose *Snap the Whip* (1872) probably did more than any other artwork to make the little red schoolhouse red in the American imagination. Depicting nine barefoot boys playing joyously in front of a bright red school, *Snap the Whip* belonged to a set of eight school-related paintings Homer produced between 1871 and 1874. The classroom interiors in Homer's images resembled the schools of his youth, with benches facing the wall instead of individual desks pointed toward the teacher. But he also painted the building red on the outside, invoking a new myth in the North about "old-time" schools. "Every person from the country knows the powerful associations lingering around the old red schoolhouse," wrote one reviewer of Homer's school series in 1872. "No spot in the whole world is so full of histories and memories." Widely reproduced as black-and-white engravings in magazines, Homer's school paintings would themselves color American memories. Even if readers could not discern the red hues in *Snap the Whip*, they readily recognized the school as a site for male camaraderie and physicality. The painting also shows a few indistinct girls in the distance, but they play quietly with a hoop while the boys run free.[14]

By the turn of the century, new forms of mass-produced entertainment—music, theater, and film—would give all these images greater scope and influence. The most successful example was the 1909 hit song "School Days," co-written by the vaudeville producer and composer Gus Edwards. Edwards had emigrated from Germany at the age of seven to Brooklyn, becoming a child prodigy and later a booking agent for other young talent, including Groucho Marx and Eddie Cantor. Yet together with Will Cobb, a native Philadelphian, Edwards wrote America's best-known paean to the rural one-room school. It follows the same basic script as Whittier's "In School Days" as the protagonists—in this case, a couple—look back at their lives and love:

School Days, School Days, dear old golden rule days
Readin' and 'ritin' and 'rithmetic
Taught to the tune of a hickory stick
You were my queen in calico
I was your bashful barefoot beau
And you wrote on my slate, "I love you Joe"
When we were a couple of kids.

But they are grown up now, and the one-room school, like the rural community that produced it, is gone forever:

'Member the meadows so green, dear
So fragrant with clover and maize,
New city lots and preferred bus'nss plots
They've cut them up since those days.

The song eventually sold more than three million copies in sheet music; in 1949, the *New York Times* ranked it as one of the ten most popular tunes of the century. "School Days" became Edwards's personal theme song, adopted for countless vaudeville "kiddie shows"—*Nine Country Kids, School Boys and School Girls, Kid Kabaret*, and so on—starring his young cast of prodigies. Rotary clubs reprinted "School Days" in their songbooks and recited it at meetings. It also inspired a 1921 movie, in which a young boy leaves the farm for the city but finally returns to his schoolhouse sweetheart.[15]

Borrowing heavily from time-worn impressions of the one-room schoolhouse, "School Days" itself spawned a slew of imitators in theater and film. Almost all these rural images were produced by city folk, many of them immigrants. A 1911 vaudeville production in Atlanta, *A Minister's Sweetheart*, was billed as "A Story of Rural New England Life"; playing on the regional stereotypes, it promised scenes in an apple orchard, a corner grocer, and a little red schoolhouse. In 1925 another Atlanta vaudeville house advertised two ventriloquists performing an "old, old entertainment in the 'The Little Red School House.'" Before he became a household name with *Birth of a Nation* (1915), meanwhile, the film director D. W. Griffith drew on similar rural themes in his movie short *The School Teacher and the Waif* (1912). Featuring an uncredited Mary Pickford as a country schoolgirl, this silent film follows the heroine as she is humiliated at a spelling bee, runs out of the schoolhouse, becomes enmeshed with a carnival huckster, and is finally rescued by her teacher and returned to school. Pickford had begun her career a few years earlier in a vaudeville traveling company, accompanied by her family; one of her first productions was entitled *The Little Red Schoolhouse*. The entire family received $20 per week for their efforts, a tiny fraction of the riches that Pickford later commanded.[16]

Sentiment, Part 2: Saluting the Nation

In most of these popular accounts, the one-room school symbolized an older, small-town America that was slowly passing away. Especially after 1890, however, another set of images tied the little red schoolhouse to the growing strength and power of the nation writ large. Adopted for the quadricentennial in 1892 of Christopher Columbus's "discovery" of the Americas, Francis Bellamy's Pledge of Allegiance made flags ubiquitous in American schools; even more, it made the school a patriotic symbol in its own right. "The Public School is the most characteristic product of the four centuries of American life [and] the source of our greatness as a nation," Bellamy told a colleague, a few months before the Columbus celebration. "It alone has made this people capable of governing themselves." The New England novelist and poet Hezekiah Butterworth produced a special verse for the occasion, "Song of the Flag," which explicitly linked these dual symbols. "Cheer, cheer we the Flag of the Nation / On Liberty's breezes unfurled," the song exulted, promising: "The school shall be true to the nation / And the nation be true to the

Right." Three years later, a local newspaper in Olympia, Washington, summarized the new American consensus on patriotic iconography. "Next to the flag," the paper declared, "the little red schoolhouse is the sign of our country."[17]

Three years after that, when the United States acquired an overseas empire, the one-room school would come to symbolize America's imperial destiny as well as its democratic virtue. In January 1899, a few months after the conclusion of the Spanish-American War, the magazine *Puck* published a cartoon showing Uncle Sam instructing his new "dark" pupils—Hawaii, Cuba, Puerto Rico, and the Philippines—in a one-room schoolhouse. "Now, children, you've got to learn these lessons whether you want to or not!" Uncle Sam chides, introducing his "new class in Civilization." Across the nation's colonial possessions, Americans quickly established public school systems; indeed, no twentieth-century empire evinced greater concern for education than the United States. So artists devoted heavy attention to new overseas schools, which became literal as well as metaphoric embodiments of the American imperial project. One drawing showed Uncle Sam reading a textbook to happy Filipino children beneath a sign announcing the arrival of American teachers on the islands. Only an 1899 cartoon in *Judge* betrayed any suggestion that some Filipinos were less than happy with the Americans. Against a panoply of American-style one-room schools—complete with bell towers and U.S. flags—the artist showed the rebel leader Emilio Aguinaldo running away. "The American school-house in the Philippines will destroy superstition, ignorance, vice, etc.," the caption predicted, "and eventually end the war and bring civilization." It would take another three years, and 250,000 Filipino lives, before the United States subdued Aguinaldo and conquered the Philippines.[18]

To be sure, the one-room school had also appeared in depictions of imperial conquest in the American West. Most prominent was the Currier and Ives lithograph *Across the Continent: Westward the Course of Empire Takes Its Way* (1868), which showed "civilization" in the form of the railroad, the telegraph, a church, and a log-cabin one-room school moving across a vast open plain. But the one-room-school image became ubiquitous in the era of overseas empire, when artists substituted the tidy clapboard of the village for the rustic logs of the frontier. Most of all, they made America's imperial schoolhouse red. A widely reproduced 1901 cartoon in *Judge* played with this color scheme, showing Uncle Sam as a truant officer hauling a Filipino child into "the little Red, White, and Blue Schoolhouse." But most imperial spokesmen simply referred to the schoolhouse as red, cementing it as a symbol of U.S. global power. "It is to the little red schoolhouse . . . that we must go to find the sceptre of the American dominion," wrote the British journalist W. T. Stead in his popular 1901 tract *The Americanization of the World*. "In America everybody, from the richest to the poorest, considers that education is a boon, a necessity of life." A Dallas newspaper echoed Stead, noting that America was now spreading its gospel of education to other lands. "Do you not agree that the American Government is right in opening up the little red schoolhouse wherever the Stars and Stripes are raised?" the paper asked.[19]

In reality, America's colonial schools were even less likely to be red than one-room schools back home. Most new schools in the Philippines were made of wood and leaves from nipa, an indigenous palm tree. "As an edifying influence in its own sphere," one American teacher bragged, "the nipa school-house of the Philippines bids fair to outdo its prototype, the 'little red schoolhouse' of the United States." More commonly, however, Americans referred to their overseas schools, like their domestic ones, as red. Praising local resident William Banish for serving as "one of Uncle Sam's teachers" in the Philippines, a North Dakota newspaper noted that he taught "amid tropical foliage" in a nipa school. "Mr. Banish encloses a photograph of his school—the little red school house—ever the herald of civilization," the newspaper added, as if a black-and-white photo could reveal the school's real color. Likewise, a Miami paper praised the little red school and soap—"the real advance agent of civilization"—for educating Filipinos in self-government. Even outside their own empire, Americans invoked the red school image in their tributes to education. A businessman in Mexico urged Latin America to build ten thousand little red schoolhouses, from the Rio Grande to Patagonia, and in China a missionary warned that only the red schoolhouse could block the spread of the red flag (communism) from East Asia.[20]

Even as the one-room school symbolized America's global expansion, it would also be summoned by Americans who wanted to seal off the nation from the rest of the world. In 1871 the cartoonist Thomas Nast showed the school under assault from crocodiles shaped like Catholic prelates; inside the classroom, meanwhile, a simian-looking Irish boy threatened the teacher ("Miss Columbia") with a dagger, a pistol, and a bottle of rum. By the 1890s nativist groups like the American Protective Association had adopted the little red schoolhouse as their official insignia. In 1894, the APA presented a friendly congressman with a two-foot floral arrangement in the shape of a red schoolhouse, complete with a bell at the top. The following year, APA marchers joined with other nativists behind a Little Red Schoolhouse float in the Boston Fourth of July parade: Uncle Sam stood in the doorway, men read books in the three windows, and the roof was capped with a U.S. flag. Riots ensued, sparked by Catholic onlookers who took offense at the schoolhouse display. "By this symbol," one acute British observer wrote, "the descendants of the Pilgrim Fathers of New England showed that they were still decidedly opposed to the interference of any other 'fathers' in the management of their public schools." A few months later, and a continent away, San Francisco's APA warned "Roman Catholic hordes" against "meddling" with the schools.[21]

Well before the color red became associated with Communism, indeed, nativists linked it to Catholicism. "The Baptist does not believe in the red hat, but does believe in the little red schoolhouse," declared a Baptist leader in 1895, warning against "papal" influences in education. Such fears decreased during the first decades of the twentieth century but revived in the 1920s, when the Ku Klux Klan mounted an all-out assault on American Catholics. Blocking Catholic demands for state subsidies to parochial schools, the KKK also sought to bar children from attending these schools at all. Its own parade floats featured crosses and horsemen—the standard Klan regalia—along with the Bible, the American flag, and the little red schoolhouse. "The Klan Goes Marching On, Warning of the Dangers That Threaten Our Republic," declared one KKK parade banner, draped over a red school. In its publications, too, the Klan used the red schoolhouse to underscore the "red peril" of Catholicism. One illustration depicted a KKK angel with a sword defending the school from a devil marked "Rome"; another showed a Klansman on a horse, standing guard at the humble one-room school.[22]

Predictably, then, the little red schoolhouse also appeared in political campaigns whenever questions of immigration, ethnicity, and education arose. Republicans in Wisconsin harnessed the image to defend the Bennett Law of 1889, which required private as well as public schools to teach in the English language. Fearful of losing its legislative majority to the Democrats, who rallied German voters against the measure, the state GOP devised a party emblem of a one-room school with the motto "Stand by It!" Republicans sent the symbol to newspapers, affixed it to buttons and badges, and pictured GOP Governor William Hoard next to it. "'Hoard and the Little School House' will be the watchword of the campaign," one Republican newspaper predicted, "a reminder of the days [in 1840] when William Henry Harrison swept the country by the magic of the words 'Tippecanoe' and 'The Old Log Cabin.'" But Democrats, perhaps recalling their drubbing in Harrison's log-cabin campaign, refused to let the GOP monopolize the one-room school. They adopted the same emblem and added a new motto: "All the Schools." The maneuver signaled their support for private schools "and the right of every parent to direct the education of his child," as one party operative explained. With the help of the schoolhouse symbol, Democrats soon recaptured the Wisconsin statehouse and repealed the Bennett Law.[23]

In the wake of Boston's "Little Red Schoolhouse" riots of 1895, likewise, Massachusetts Republicans chose the red school as their icon; in response, Democrats designed a white school emblem of their own. After that, parties tended to eschew ethnic allusions in their schoolhouse imagery. The one-room school became a free-floating signifier, connecting candidates to the simplicity of the past—and the prosperity of the future. In 1896, GOP posters for William McKinley featured a picture of a one-room school alongside drawings of booming factories, prosperous farms, and the other alleged benefits of the tariff. "Our Home Defenders," the poster blared: just as Republicans had guarded the American school, it seemed, so would they protect American industries. Seeking to exploit their candidate's small-town Vermont image, advocates for Calvin Coolidge briefly used the little red schoolhouse as a symbol in his 1924 campaign. Ironically, Coolidge favored consolidated schools; as one wag suggested, the chimney on the GOP emblem probably burned green wood in a decrepit second-hand stove. Angry Coolidge supporters eventually dropped the symbol when they discovered that it had been introduced by a sly button manufacturer who was trying to drum up campaign revenue by "capitalizing the idea" of the little red schoolhouse.[24]

Across the business world, of course, advertisers and salesmen did exactly that. As early as 1884, the Chicago-based Henderson Company—"Sole Agents" of Little Red School House Shoes—affixed the icon to every pair it sold. Like the one-room school itself, the company promised, its shoes were "made on common sense ideas." An 1897 Henderson advertisement played on racial stereotypes as well as school nostalgia, picturing "darkie" students reciting to their teacher: "We are happy little children / We love our pleasant school / We love our gentle teacher / And obey his 12-inch rule." A New Jersey manufacturer of laboratory beakers published a promotional booklet in 1908 entitled "The Little Red School House," showing the "men and women of Achievement" who had received their early education there: Benjamin Franklin, Horace Mann, Henry David Thoreau, Henry Clay, and others. Never mind that some of these luminaries—especially Mann—were bitter critics of the one-room school, or that the advertised product would never have been used there.

Similarly, a school-supply company hawking auditorium seats and other modern devices decorated its catalogue with a one-room school. Regardless of how new the item being sold, it could only benefit from connections to the old red school.[25]

In some cases, finally, corporations even constructed full-scale replicas of the little red schoolhouse to market their wares. One of the first businesses to do so was the advertising industry itself, which erected a school outside the hall where its 1917 annual convention was being held: since advertising was inherently educational, an announcement explained, the little red schoolhouse was "The Birthplace of All Advertising." In Atlanta a department store put up a "real, honest-to-goodness Little Red Schoolhouse" to promote its back-to-school sales. Children accompanied by their mothers—potential customers—were invited to sing "School Days" and other "familiar airs" inside the makeshift building, adding "a real school touch" to the event. Yet the real little red schoolhouse was gone forever, as a second Atlanta department store countered in its own back-to-school advertisement. Like the "old Country store," the copy noted, the one-room school had served an important purpose. "But today the scene has changed a bit," it continued. "Progress has marched down the line at a merry clip." Just as grand department stores had replaced the single-family enterprise, so had large consolidated schools supplanted the little red schoolhouse. Once upon a time, the one-room school symbolized progress. Now it stood in the way, an outdated carryover from long ago.[26]

The Struggle for School Consolidation

Out in the countryside many Americans did not agree. They still shopped at the village store, and they still defended the one-room school. In the struggle over school consolidation, indeed, rural Americans drew on all the same images that poets, painters, politicians, and advertisers had created. In Wisconsin they even revived the GOP's Bennett Law symbol—a one-room school with the motto "Stand by It"—in an effort to stave off larger, mixed-district schools. Appropriating popular representations of the little red schoolhouse, rural activists simultaneously invoked local and national identities: as one upstate New Yorker argued, school consolidators "had no conception of what the little red schoolhouse had meant in the lives of thousands of men and women and to the nation as a whole." It was left to Progressives to fight the one-room school—and to challenge the romantic images surrounding it. "Alas, for the sentiment which has so long hallowed the little old New England school!" declared a frustrated educator in Texas. "It played an important part in our early history. . . . But sentiment must yield to economic necessity."[27]

Progressivism was a complex and diverse reform movement, encompassing everything from forest conservation and meat inspection to playgrounds and juvenile courts. Most of all, the Progressives shared a powerful faith in education itself: by creating and disseminating new forms of knowledge, they believed, reformers could bring forth the new regulations and systems that modern society demanded. To promote school consolidation advocates released a massive barrage of statistics, testimonies, and photographs about the evils of the little red schoolhouse. Compared to their consolidated cousins, one-room schools were unsanitary: students contracted tuberculosis from the dirty air, suffered spinal injuries from the backless benches, and damaged their eyesight trying to work in the poor lighting. Even more, Progressives argued, one-room schools failed to teach: relying mostly on rote and the rod, America's country educators ignored the latest techniques of learning by doing. Unfortunately, the bulk of rural Americans seemed satisfied with the status quo. "As it is now, the country school sits in the valley of the shadow of ignorance, awaiting patiently the time of its redemption," declared an Iowa educator in 1890, on the cusp of the first consolidation campaigns. To save rural America, a California school official added, Progressives would have to protect rural citizens from themselves.[28]

The only way to do that, the Californian added, was via publicity. In Colorado, state educational officials distributed postcards showing six ramshackle one-room schools beneath a stark caption, "A National Disgrace"; in Ohio, they conducted house-to-house canvasses and mass mailings; and in Oklahoma, they adopted a new letterhead with the words, "The Better Chance: Consolidated Schools." Lest readers miss the point, the letterhead featured two sets of drawings. In "The Old Way," students walked to an ugly one-room school; in "The New Way," they rode a bus to an attractive, multistoried building. At the national level, meanwhile, the U.S. Department of Agriculture produced a two-thousand-foot "film picture" (as it was called) showing children being picked up by horse-drawn carriages and entering a large, well-appointed school. Once they got inside, the girls studied cooking and sewing while the boys learned new techniques in agriculture and animal husbandry. The message to rural America was clear: instead of destroying country traditions, the consolidated school would protect and improve them. Indeed, one prominent advocate insisted, newly centralized schools promised nothing less than "the complete regeneration of rural life."[29]

As the Progressives correctly sensed, this argument could easily backfire. On the one hand, consolidated schools would overcome the inequity and inefficiency of the one-room school; on the other, they would revive the communal spirit and energy that had infused the little red schoolhouse. To square an attack on the schoolhouse with a defense of it, the Progressives fell back on progress itself. At one time, they conceded, the one-room school had played a key role. "In an earlier day the one-teacher school was more vital to country life," two consolidation advocates in Delaware wrote. "The district school had life and movement, staged running matches, jumping contests, fistic encounters, wrestling bouts, and battles royal behind snowy breastworks." Like it nor not, however, that era was over. "Gone are these days and gone is this district school; gone as irretrievably as the country mill and the miller's daughter. Modern education, even in small schools, is less romantic and more businesslike, more formal, more exact, more specialized, done according to tested methods and a standard schedule." Like the spinning wheel and the oxcart, a Connecticut educator proclaimed, the "little red school house of past generations" would have to yield to "improvement and progress."[30]

To demonstrate this inevitable process, reformers often employed a favorite Progressive technique: the historical pageant. Across America towns and cities staged elaborate plays and parades to connect the glory of the past with the promise of the future. One-room schools held a conspicuous place in these rituals, reminding the community of how far it had come. For the Indiana State Centennial of 1915, Bartholomew County designed a pageant that began with several features of "pioneer life," including a cornhusking and a one-room school. It proceeded through the Civil War—complete with actual bugles, fifes, and drums—and concluded with a modern school, the ultimate symbol of progress. In nearby Muncie, made famous by the sociologists Robert and Helen Lynd, another pageant started with a "little pioneer school" and ended with scenes from "a flourishing modern city." At their 1920 meeting in Cleveland, meanwhile, the National Education Association's Department of Superintendents watched five hundred local students stage a pageant about schooling itself. "The old time school in which the 'rule of the rod' prevailed was shown," wrote one witness, "in pleasing contrast to the modern school of the best type." Needless to say, the old-time school had just one room; the modern institution was consolidated.[31]

As the Progressives would discover, however, millions of Americans resisted the siren song of modernity. The more the reformers made the consolidated school into a symbol of progress, indeed, the more some citizens rallied against it. For urban and rural dwellers alike, the little red schoolhouse became an emblem for the old-time virtues that modern society—especially modern education—had forgotten. True, a California journalist wrote in 1907, the one-room school was "crude, even rude" in its construction and facilities. But it did its job well—much better, in fact, than contemporary schools did.

> There was a thorough, often painful, drill in the fundamentals. The little rustics were not taught to prance about on a stage, nor were they given a smattering of all the "oligies," just enough to fill them with conceit of themselves and contempt of their elders, but they were made to know, and know thoroughly, how to read, to spell, to write, and to cipher; also they were made to know their geography, their English grammar, and the outlines of their own country at least. Let smart educators, with all their modern equipment and pretentious pedagogics, sneer as they may, it yet remains true that the immense majority of the men and women who made America, made what is sound, wholesome, and enduring in it, came out of these rustic schools.

When schools consolidated, another Californian editorialized, they became too easy. In place of the "mental discipline" of the little red schoolhouse, the modern school substituted "educational coddling" like gym class and motion pictures. "It would be instructive to match the graduate of the modern peptonized school course with a boy from the old-time little red school house," the editorial concluded, "in a test of actual mental capacity."[32]

But when educational officials did match students, administering content and I.Q. tests to urban and rural children, they found that one-room students fell short. Predictably enough, advocates for the one-room school next took aim at the tests themselves. "Educators and others are facing a grave danger in that they are becoming measuring sticks," warned one critic in *The Little Red Schoolhouse*, upstate New Yorkers' anti-consolidation journal. "We are now trying to measure brains and skulls of children by psychological tests. We are branding them for life and pre-determining their destiny." Indeed, he concluded, modern schools posed the danger of "too much efficiency." A favorite Progressive theme, "efficiency" became one of the demons of the campaign against consolidation; like its close rhetorical cousin "bureaucracy," efficiency conjured up a bloodless, impersonal system that buried small-town traditions and idiosyncrasies in a maze of regulations and policies. "Individuality will be lost, the pride taken in 'our' school and 'our' teacher gone," wrote a self-identified "Rural Mother" in New York. "Haven't the parents who bear the children anything to say? Must they yield those children up to be educated as some man or men with certain ideas in their heads, deem best?" Under consolidation, *The Little Red Schoolhouse* added, parents would cede their power to anonymous "autocrats" and "bureaucrats" in burgeoning school systems. "Bureaucracy," its headline trumpeted, "Is the Worst Form of Tyranny."[33]

Most of all, *The Little Red Schoolhouse* argued, the new emphasis upon "material progress" blinded Americans to the real purpose of education: developing "Christian character." By 1928, one columnist for the journal wrote, schools could boast "splendid buildings" and "high scores of efficiency." But crime and sexual immorality continued to flourish, suggesting that "scientific education" had "outstripped our spiritual attainments." The critique fit easily into the era's escalating campaigns against evolution and communism, which both drew freely on one-room-school imagery. As a Connecticut parent told his school board, the little red schoolhouse produced "only a very small percentage" of the "evolutionists, false scientists, schemers, socialists, bolshevists, radicals, and reds" who were bedeviling America. The rest were spawned by large consolidated schools, which themselves reflected a "Red" drift in national life. In the days of the one-room school, another parent wrote, Americans took care of themselves. But the modern school inoculated children against smallpox, examined them for eyestrain, inspected their food, and supervised their digestion. "The trend is clearly socialistic," he concluded. "It is weakening the sturdy American individualism."[34]

Such charges provoked a mix of mirth and rage among Progressive reformers, who correctly noted that many radical movements preceded school consolidation; if anything, one New Yorker wrote, "the little red schoolhouse . . . hatched the bug of Bolshevism in America" by exposing children to poor and inequitable conditions. Most of all, the Progressives took aim at the distortion of those conditions by rural activists who would not—or could not—acknowledge them. "The Little Red Schoolhouse a 'Fake,'" headlined the Progressive-leaning *Independent*, introducing a 1913 article on one-room schools in Wisconsin. As the article reported, most of the schools lacked adequate heat, light, desks, and outhouses. "There has been a great deal of speechmaking wasted on the 'little red schoolhouse, the cradle of our liberties, etc.,'" the *Independent* complained. "The splendid record of the country school in turning out leaders of the people does not make soap and water unnecessary, and the ghosts of departed statesmen do not stop cracks in the floor." As another Wisconsin critic noted, many outstanding men in politics, science, and industry were reared in the American countryside. But it did not follow that the country school rendered them outstanding.[35]

Here critics targeted the most widespread claim on behalf of the one-room school: that its heroic roster of graduates proved its worth. "Look at Abraham Lincoln and a host of other great men; they never had a newfangled school with all its frills and furbelows to go to," argued one Kansas farmer, in a typical refrain. "If a one-room school was good enough for them why isn't it good enough for us?" Much of this hype was fueled by politicians themselves, who recognized the electoral value of a red school pedigree; as a Kansas City newspaper wryly noted, it marked a candidate as "a self-made man who began at the grassroots." It also led politicians to distort their own biographies: starting in 1923, for example, Herbert Hoover falsely claimed that he had attended a one-room school. As Progressives often noted, this entire charade gave the one-room school more credit than it deserved. "Great men have issued from the 'little red school house,' it is true, but they have become great men not because but in spite of the fact that the school house was 'little' and was 'red,'" wrote one North Dakota educator. Seeking to prove the point, school consolidators conducted a study of the 1924 edition of *Who's Who in America*. Although 70 percent of Americans lived on farms in 1870, the study noted, only 25 percent of the people in *Who's Who* were born on a farm—or, presumably, educated in a one-room school.[36]

Sentimentalism Reborn

By this time the one-room school had already begun its rapid decline. Between 1918 and 1928, roughly forty thousand American single-teacher schools (one-fifth of the total) closed their doors; over the next decade, a similar number would shut down as well. In Mississippi, two-thirds of white rural schools closed between 1910 and 1924. Meanwhile, the number of consolidated schools in the state rose from two to eighty-six. To be sure, angry pockets of resistance remained. In rural East Lincoln, Mississippi, the principal of a new consolidated school was shot and killed; the following year his successor was stabbed and nearly died. Nevertheless, Progressives could confidently predict the final demise of the little red schoolhouse. "This relic, while not yet extinct, is plainly destined to follow the dodo into oblivion," one New Yorker wrote. "The one-room schoolhouse with its inevitable belfry and flagpole cannot long endure." Indeed, a North Carolina journalist happily added, its bells were "tolling their dying dirge."[37]

Yet these same Progressives also evinced a note of sadness about this development, reflecting their own nostalgic attachment to the rural one-room school. In the movement for social centers, especially, reformers decried the decline of the little red schoolhouse and struggled to re-create its tight-knit community in an urban setting. To the Rochester minister Edward J. Ward, the leading figure in this movement, the one-room school embodied the "man-to-man frankness" American cities had forsaken. "There was a spirit of neighborhood there," Ward wrote, "not only in the sociables, the spelldowns, and singing school, but in the meetings where folks just listened to speakers and talked." By opening their doors to adult recreation and education, he argued, urban schools could revive the collective spirit of their rural predecessors. Ward would help forge a national organization, the Social Center Association of America, which began its meetings with a wistful song:

Come close and let us wake the joy
Our fathers used to know
When to the little schoolhouse
Together they would go
Then neighbor's heart to neighbor warmed
In thought for common good
We'll strike the fine old chord again
A song of neighborhood

Of course, as one social-center advocate admitted, one-room schools were closed most evenings and throughout the summer vacation; however "embalmed in story and song," the small rural school had never served the broad communal function that its new urban enthusiasts imagined. Even Ward acknowledged as much, underlining the obvious distortions that nostalgia could produce. "There is something strange . . . about this memory of how *we* used to get together," Ward wrote of the one-room school. "Men *remember* it who never actually knew the spontaneous common centering of the old days. Younger men *remember* it who have always lived in the city."[38]

Out in the countryside, meanwhile, a handful of Progressives began a quiet but quixotic campaign to revive the little red schoolhouse itself. Like antievolutionists and other rural conservatives, these reformers condemned bureaucrats and state politicians for consolidating single-teacher schools. Whereas the conservatives envisioned the one-room school as a site of strict discipline and rote learning, however, Progressives praised it as the wellspring of their own favored pedagogy: "progressive education." Associated most strongly with Maria Montessori in Europe and John Dewey in the United States, progressive education held that schooling should be child-centered, not teacher-centered; active, not passive; and based in experience, not simply in books. In most historical accounts, the one-room school embodied the antithesis of this philosophy. Yet by the mid-1920s, the *New York Times* observed, some progressive educators had begun to rethink their long-standing rejection of the little red schoolhouse. Unlike students in large urban high schools and consolidated rural schools, who obtained an impersonal "mass education," pupils in the one-room school received individual attention and recognition. Each child could advance at his or her own pace; even more, all the children—and their parents—knew each other. "The little red schoolhouse [is] coming into its own again," the *Times* reported. "In a nation prone everywhere to substitute mass products for quality, it is an example of wide applicability."[39]

Here the *Times* cited the novelist and educator Dorothy Canfield Fisher, the most prominent voice in this rural-school reassessment. In her best-selling children's book, *Understood Betsy* (1916), Fisher told the story of a nervous, unhealthy city girl who finds strength and happiness in the rustic hills of Vermont. Entering the local one-room school, Betsy is shocked to discover that she has not been assigned to a grade. "She always thought she was [in school] to pass from one grade to another, and she was ever so startled to get a little glimpse of the fact that she was there to learn how to read and write and cipher and generally use her mind." Compounding Betsy's surprise, a local farmer stops by the school during recess to play with the children; back in the city, grownups never did that. "They never even looked at the children, any more than if they were in another world," Fisher explained. "In fact, [Betsy] had felt the school was another world." Respecting the individual but connecting her to the community, Betsy's one-room school was a near-perfect embodiment of progressive education. It especially reflected the influence of Montessori, whom Fisher visited in Rome in 1911. Returning home, she produced several "how-to" guides to Montessori as well as the fictional tribute to her in *Understood Betsy.* If Americans understood Montessorian principles, Fisher wrote, they might reject the "hierarchic rigidity" of modern education and rejuvenate the one-room school.[40]

Fisher also tried to apply these principles in her own life, moving back to Vermont, where she had summered as a child, and enrolling her children in the same one-room school her great-grandfather had attended. Like many rural schools, it was in dire need of physical renovation. So Fisher organized a historical pageant to raise money for the school, depicting life "as it was" when Vermont joined the union in 1791. Whereas most Progressive pageants concluded with a "modern" consolidated school, however, Fisher's drama ended where it began: with the little red schoolhouse. All it required was a fresh coat of paint and some basic repairs, Fisher wrote, which would transform the "dreary little schoolhouse" into an attractive, homelike school. "Progress goes traditionally in a spiral, not in a straight course," Fisher wrote in 1916, the same year she published *Understood Betsy*. "Its great circling sweep has brought it around again to a point where the much-despised country school offers the best of all possible fields for reconstruction along the most modern and advanced lines." Everything old was new again, or should be: to create a more progressive educational future, Americans need only look back to their rural past.[41]

In most parts of the nation, however, one-room schools were already gone. Living in Vermont, Fisher might credibly call upon her neighbors to protect and patronize the little red schoolhouse. Elsewhere, though, the only way to experience a one-room school was to restore an abandoned one as a historic or museum site. Starting in the 1920s, Americans who shared an attachment to these schools began to refurbish them for tourists. The best candidates were places where a famous individual had taught, promising to lure more visitors than a generic one-room building. New Jersey education officials purchased the empty school where Red Cross founder Clara Barton taught, raising money across the state to refurbish it: every teacher was asked to donate five cents to the cause, while students were asked to give a penny each. Spearheaded by the poet Edna St. Vincent Millay, a group of well-known New York writers raised funds to preserve Walt Whitman's one-room school on Long Island. And in Connecticut the philanthropist Arthur J. Silliman left $400,000—a vast sum at the time—to "perpetuate the one-room red schoolhouse" where Nathan Hale had served as master after he left Yale, before he was martyred in the American Revolution.[42]

The most famous restorer of one-room schools was the automobile titan Henry Ford, who reconstructed schools at the Wayside Inn in Sudbury, Massachusetts (made famous by the poet Henry Wadsworth Longfellow), and at his own historical village in Dearborn, Michigan. The school at Wayside was moved from nearby Sterling, where it had supposedly served as the site for the episode that inspired the children's poem "Mary Had a Little Lamb": young Mary Elizabeth Sawyer had brought a lamb to school and teacher John Roulstone informed her that "it was against the rule." The poem was a favorite of Ford's and also of his close associate Thomas Edison, who recorded it as the first words on the phonograph he invented. In Michigan, Ford rebuilt the one-room school from his own rural childhood. At least thirty other family members, including Ford's mother, had attended the Scotch Settlement School, which Ford had transported, brick by brick, to his historical Greenfield Village in Dearborn. A stickler for detail, Ford made sure that the school's stove and coal-oil lamps were placed in their exact previous locations. But he also installed a modern furnace (conveniently out of sight in the basement) and put in electric lights, hidden behind the original moldings.[43]

Most astonishing, Ford also paid for students to attend both these restored schools and for teachers to instruct them. To Ford, like Dorothy Canfield Fisher, the one-room school epitomized the Progressive philosophy of learning by doing. Instead of preserving them as dry museum pieces, then, Ford tried to make the schools into object lessons —another favorite Progressive cliché—of active, experience-based education. At the 1927 opening of the Wayside school, for example, Ford directed the reenactment of its famous poem, complete with a girl named Mary and a live, very frisky lamb. At Greenfield Village he personally greeted each of the thirty-two children who started at his refurbished school in 1929. Then Ford entered the school with an old classmate, who had come for the ceremony, and each man carved his initials at the spot where he used to sit. Ford was a frequent visitor to the Scotch Settlement School after that, delighting especially in the students' pranks against the teachers he had hired. After the pupils discovered that soybeans from Ford's nearby farm were perfect ammunition for peashooters, their instructors banned the beans from the classroom. But Ford loved the skirmishes between student and teacher, which reminded him of the disciplinary battles of his own youth. So he secretly brought the children bags of soybeans, which were—like Mary's lamb—against the rule.[44]

Ironically, Henry Ford had probably done more than any American to rid the nation of one-room schools. When rural Americans traveled by horseback or wagon over mud roads, as the Michigan political scientist Thomas H. Reed explained, they often had little choice but to attend one-room schools. Only after Ford ushered in his "revolution in wheels" did bigger schools become possible. Indeed, to promote their products the auto industries frequently lobbied for school consolidation. In 1920, for example, the Firestone Truck and Rubber Company distributed a pamphlet highlighting the "defects" of the one-room school and the educational advantages of consolidated ones. Needless to say, this arrangement would work to Firestone's advantage, as well: as the pamphlet pointed out, the new schools would require school buses and improved roads to handle them. "Good roads and good consolidated schools go hand in hand—one is the inevitable complement of the other," Firestone proclaimed. Even as the world's greatest auto manufacturer worked to restore the little red schoolhouse, it seemed, the world that he created was ensuring its demise. Americans drove their cars and buses right past the one-room school, which would soon exist only in their imaginations.[45]

One of the eight new entrances to the Department of Education
erected in 2002 to promote the No Child Left Behind law
(photograph by Bryan Cannon)

Teenagers in a one-room school in Breathitt
County, Kentucky, in 1940 enjoy a box supper in which the
boys bid on meals prepared anonymously by the girls, after which
the winners share their meal with the cooks (Farm Security Administration Collection, Library of Congress Prints and Photographs
Division, Washington, D.C., LC-USF34-055786-D,
courtesy of the Library of Congress)

A schoolhouse for white children in Grundy
County, Iowa, in 1939 (top) and its counterpart for black
children in Destrehan County, Louisiana, in 1938 highlight the
differences in the public education offered to whites and blacks
(Farm Security Administration Collection, Library of Congress
Prints and Photographs Division, Washington, D.C.,
LC-USF34-028414-D and LC-DIG-fsa-8a23544,
courtesy of the Library of Congress)

Winslow Homer's widely reproduced *Snap the Whip* (1872)
probably did more than any other image to make the one-room
schoolhouse red in the public imagination (Collection of the
Butler Institute of American Art, Youngstown, Ohio)

Whether in the frontier West or in the
Philippines, the little red schoolhouse served as a
powerful symbol of American imperial expansion, as seen in
Currier and Ives's *Across the Continent: Westward the Course of Empire
Takes Its Way* (1868) (top; drawn by F. F. Palmer, Library of Congress,
Washington, D.C., LC-DIG-ppmsca-03213, courtesy of the
Library of Congress), and Louis Dalrymple's "School Begins,"
from *Puck*, 25 January 1899 (color lithograph by Louis
Dalrymple, copyrighted by Keppler & Schwarzmann,
courtesy of the Library of Congress)

THE AMERICAN RIVER GANGES.

Thomas Nast's "The American River Ganges,"
which appeared in *Harper's Weekly*, September 1871,
used the one-room schoolhouse to depict white Protestants
as under siege from Irish Catholics (Library of Congress
Prints and Photographs Division, Washington, D.C.,
courtesy of the Library of Congress)

In a 1940 series of photographs from Breathitt
County, Kentucky, photographer Marion Post Wolcott
contrasted the dilapidation of one-room schools (top) with the
superior facilities found in consolidated schools (Farm Security
Administration Collection, Library of Congress Prints and
Photographs Division, Washington, D.C., LC-USF
34-055907-D and LC-USF34-055988-D,
courtesy of the Library of Congress)

PENNSYLVANIA
THE LITTLE RED SCHOOLHOUSE

This Katherine Milhous poster, created in the
late 1930s, idealized an Amish one-room schoolhouse,
reflecting Americans' ambivalence about progress and modernity
(Works Project Administration Poster Collection, Library of Congress
Prints and Photographs Division, Washington, D.C., LC-USZC2-
5670, courtesy of the Library of Congress)

E. M. Root's 1953 pamphlet "How Red Is the Little Red
Schoolhouse?" was part of the conservative Cold War campaign
against Communist subversion (courtesy of Robert Donner Collection,
Brown Library, Abilene Christian University, Abilene, Texas)

This Parker Brothers board game, created in 1952, joined a slew of similarly themed commercial products in the 1950s, including Little Red Schoolhouse clocks, toys, and bookbags (photograph by Todd Bressi)

THREE

From Poverty to Democracy

In 1940 the New Deal photographer John Vachon outlined the subjects he hoped to capture on film in the coming year. As a member of the Information Division of the Farm Security Administration, Vachon wrote, his first task was to depict "underprivileged people" across rural America. But he also sought to tell "Stories of American Institutions," including courthouses, stores, barbershops, and most of all schools. Working mainly in the Midwest, Vachon resolved to dramatize the differences between "inadequate" one-room schools and newer, consolidated buildings. Later that year, a second FSA photographer underlined the same goal in the pictures and captions she sent from rural Kentucky. "Most of the children have no shoes and insufficient clothing to walk the long distance over bad roads and up creek beds," wrote Marion Post Wolcott beneath a photo of barefoot students on their way to school. She also took hundreds of pictures of one-room schools, highlighting their "overcrowded conditions and need for repairs and equipment." Wolcott concluded the shoot with photos of the region's new consolidated school, an attractive stone building that stood in stark contrast to its decrepit single-room predecessors.[1]

Fifteen years later, in the midst of the Cold War, a similar tableau of school photographs provoked a congressional outcry. In 1954 the United States Information Agency bought nearly thirty thousand copies of *Profile of America*, a colorful book of photographs, which the agency sent around the world to illustrate the case for democracy. But when the USIA applied the following year for funds to translate and distribute two hundred thousand more copies of the book, Congress balked. Lawmakers especially objected to a picture on page 307 of an antiquated one-room school, captioned "Little Red Schoolhouse, 1750," which allegedly opened America to criticism from its Communist foes. It made little difference that nearby pages depicted a "modern high school" and Harvard University, underscoring educational progress since the birth of the republic. Nor did a foreword by the super-patriot and aeronautics hero Charles Lindbergh quell congressional concerns. The mere portrayal of a one-room school—small, primitive, and unadorned—provided ample propaganda value for the nation's enemies. If the country did not watch out, critics warned, the Reds would use the little red schoolhouse against it.[2]

Together these passages highlight the key mid-century transition in American conceptions of the one-room schoolhouse. The country still had more than a hundred thousand one-room schools by the late 1930s, when journalists and educators, armed with New Deal photographs, turned them into symbols of rural poverty and injustice. Like the Progressives before them, New Deal critics condemned the single-teacher school as a holdover from a premodern era; by sentencing children to lives of deprivation, the critics said, these schools also violated America's founding ideals of equality and opportunity. When the nation entered World War II, however, it transformed the one-room school into an emblem of democracy. To a New Yorker speaking in 1942, the little red schoolhouse symbolized "the endurance of our ideals and our institutions," and to Missouri educators writing three years later, it was largely responsible for the defeat of fascism. "Without the far reaching influence of this rural institution," they wrote, "there is a grave question whether our democratic form of government would have survived." Rather than staining American principles, in short, the one-room school embodied them. And with these principles under fire, Americans rallied to the symbol, if not the reality, of the little red schoolhouse.[3]

In the 1950s, when the nation faced a new Communist foe, symbol and reality became almost entirely disconnected. Thanks to the war and subsequent baby boom, more than four-fifths of America's one-room schools closed their doors; in 1960, just 1 percent of students attended a single-teacher school. In the face of the Soviet challenge, meanwhile, the little red schoolhouse assumed new, unprecedented ideological importance. Politicians, diplomats, and educators celebrated the single-room school as the lodestar of American strength and freedom; across the country local communities began to restore these abandoned buildings as "a monument to nostalgia," as one skeptical reporter observed. Indeed, the anthropologist Margaret Mead noted, the disappearance of the one-room school made it even more important in America's collective memory. "The little red schoolhouse, which exists today only in backwards and forgotten areas of the country, is still the symbol of a stable, democratic, slowly changing, real American world," Mead told a Harvard lecture audience in 1950. "This image . . . crops up in the minds of those who have never in fact seen such a school, so firmly is it rooted in our literature and tradition. Like so many symbols of the American dream, it stands for a desirable state never attained and for a past golden age which has been lost."[4] It also stood for the challenges of the future, as an anxious nation steeled itself for a long struggle with its Soviet rival. Decrepit and nearly extinct, the real one-room school was of little use in this epic battle; indeed, as the USIA controversy illustrated, it might even help the enemy. So Americans called upon an imaginary little red schoolhouse, which would stiffen the nation's backbone in its time of greatest need.

A New Deal for the One-Room School

In December 1928, a thousand well-wishers gathered in Warm Springs, Georgia, to honor the new governor-elect of New York. Speaking at his countryside retreat, Franklin D. Roosevelt gave the crowd an optimistic picture of the years to come. Adopting "the idea of modernity and progress as a sort of text," the *New York Times* reported, Roosevelt predicted that farmers would harness new scientific methods of agriculture, the radio and automobile would dampen "sectional feeling," states would build better roads, and all these factors would help replace one-room schoolhouses with larger, consolidated institutions. Contemporary life was so complex, Roosevelt said, that it "required more up-to-date methods of education than those of the little red schoolhouse." Bursting into applause, the audience offered its own prediction: that Roosevelt would soon move from Albany to Washington. "Roosevelt Hailed as 1932 President," the *Times* headline blared.[5]

In the short term, at least, the crowd proved more prescient than their hero. Roosevelt swept into the White House in 1932, buoyed not by "modernity and progress" but by the worst economic crisis the country had ever witnessed. The Great Depression took an especially dire toll on rural communities and their one-room schools. Cash-strapped districts slashed teachers' salaries or paid them in "warrant," a promise of compensation at some later date; others simply closed down. America's one-room-school teachers received an average of $874 in 1931, less than half what city teachers earned; if all these impoverished instructors stood side by side, the U.S. Office of Education calculated, they would extend more than eighty-seven miles. Like urban breadlines, poor rural teachers and their ramshackle schools highlighted the fundamental inequalities of American life. "Some of our children are paupers and some are millionaires in educational opportunity," the journalist Eunice Barnard argued in 1934. "An American public school at the moment may connote anything from an unheated, dilapidated one-room shack, closed without further notice, to a 200-room palace whose frescoed walls, swimming pool, and air-conditioned interior a Roman emperor might envy." Across the country, two hundred thousand teachers were out of work; worse, three million teenagers lacked a job or a school to attend.[6]

But there was hope on the horizon, Barnard added, "thanks to the Federal Government." Here she alluded to aid from the Public Works Administration, one of the original "alphabet agencies" in Roosevelt's New Deal. Providing lump-sum grants to states and localities, the PWA would assist in constructing or improving nearly seven thousand schools. It was joined in 1935 by the Works Progress Administration, which paid laborers directly from the federal till; over the next three years, the WPA helped build more than three thousand new schools and repaired more than twenty-one thousand. By 1939 federal agencies had invested nearly $1 billion in school construction. The majority of this aid went to large urban schools or consolidated rural ones, accelerating the demise of the one-room school: although some communities wished to retain their old schoolhouses, one upstate New Yorker remarked, the lure of federal dollars was simply too great to refuse. "So the little red schoolhouse, after graduating generations of boys and girls, comes at last to its own commencement," another New York editorialist wrote, praising New Deal aid to consolidated schools. Across the countryside, to be sure, scores of one-room schools remained. But even these buildings had frequently received "a recent coat of WPA paint," the editorial quipped, "that may be any color except red."[7]

Overall, the New Deal placed a rather low premium on education: distrusting what he called "the school crowd," Roosevelt consistently rejected educators' demands for all-purpose federal aid. He preferred targeted or "emergency" relief for youth employment and especially for new school construction, which provided a more tangible illustration of his administration's achievements. In his first reelection bid, for example, Democrats released a special campaign leaflet to highlight school improvement under the New Deal. Entitled "What Happened to the Little Red Schoolhouse?" the 1936 leaflet featured a cartoon "slate" enumerating Roosevelt's accomplishments, including three thousand new or renovated schools. It also took aim at GOP challenger Alf Landon, the governor of Kansas, where education spending had plummeted to the lowest rate in the nation; in the state's nearly seven thousand single-teacher schools, some instructors received as little as $25 per month. An accompanying drawing showed two farmers at a fence with a ramshackle one-room school behind them. "Where's Alf Today?" the first farmer asks. "He's back east tellin' the folks about education!" his friend explains.[8]

After Roosevelt's reelection, ironically, New Dealers would tell a similar story about rural education in the nation writ large: it was crude, impoverished, and utterly inadequate. The key voice in this effort was the Information Division of the Farm Security Administration, which conducted a massive pictorial survey of rural American life between 1935 and 1943. Employing many of the nation's best-known photographers—including Dorothea Lange, Walker Evans, Ben Shahn, and Gordon Parks—the FSA initially set out to document the most urgent crises of the countryside, especially the Dust Bowl of the Plains states and migrant workers in the West. Even more, as Marion Post Wolcott admitted, the FSA served as a "propaganda outfit" for the New Deal itself: by depicting the problems of rural America, which were too often veiled from city folk, photographers would also dramatize the need for federal intervention and reform. Of the FSA photos that concerned education, therefore, the overwhelming majority showed one-room schools. The remainder portrayed consolidated schools, the New Deal's answer to the problem of rural education.[9]

Lest viewers miss these points, meanwhile, FSA photographers provided captions to highlight them. To be sure, some photos spoke for themselves: when a one-room school was boarded up or falling down, all that was needed was a simple title: "Ozark school building," "Abandoned schoolhouse," and the like. For shots of less decrepit buildings, however, the photographer often added words to narrate their inadequacies. "This school had five cases of scabies out of fifteen attending," wrote Russell Lee beneath his photo of a classroom in North Dakota; for a shot of rural schoolchildren in Texas, Lee noted that one of them had hookworm. In a series of school pictures from Oregon, meanwhile, he took pains to point out that the school was actually held in a church basement. "The school board didn't have adequate buses for transportation of all the children," Lee wrote, "and consequently many did not attend school." For a photo from North Carolina, likewise, Wolcott stressed the poor attendance at the school. "There were twenty children enrolled, only eight present, busy tobacco season," Wolcott wrote. Yet when she got to Kentucky, site of her most famous series, Wolcott emphasized the opposite: schools had too many students, not too few. Several of her captions drew viewers' attention to "overcrowded conditions" in the schools, especially students sitting on one another's laps. For her best-known picture, the title told the whole story: "Sharing Desks."[10]

Furthermore, although almost all the FSA photographers were white, they paid close attention to minority schools. Here, too, detailed captions were often unnecessary: photographers simply identified a one-room school as "colored" or "Negro," leaving viewers to discern the crude blackboards, crowded benches, and filthy conditions. At other times, however, photographers added words to elaborate the inadequacy—and especially the inequality—of rural black schools. "This year, despite the fact the white school received free books, none arrived for the Negros," wrote Russell Lee beneath a photo of a black classroom in Oklahoma. "The teacher was so afraid of losing her job that she would not make any inquiries about the books and the children were sharing the few books some could buy." On the same shoot, beneath a photo of black students huddled around the school stove, Lee noted that the temperature indoors that morning never rose above 50 degrees. For a series of pictures from New Mexico, similarly, photographer John Collier underscored the poor equipment and facilities of a one-room "Spanish-American" school. "The books from which the children study are selected from the public school system of Michigan, and have little relation to Spanish culture," wrote Collier, son of the famous social activist and U.S. Indian commissioner. Beneath another picture in the series, ironically, Collier took the same school to task for teaching children in their native language of Spanish and hindering their acquisition of English.[11]

Not every FSA school picture told a tale of woe. At the conclusion of her Kentucky series, for example, Marion Wolcott included a set of shots of the county's handsome new consolidated school; in a caption she praised it for introducing an "activity program" of regional arts and crafts. Even some of the one-room-school pictures depicted classic scenes of rural simplicity and pleasure, reflecting the FSA's effort to capture positive "small-town" virtues alongside images of hardship and poverty. In a photo from Morton County, North Dakota, students built a snow fort during recess; in southeast Missouri, they played tug-of-war; in Tipler, Wisconsin, they rested on the grass outside school; and in Grundy County, Iowa, they waved good-bye to their teacher as they walked home. Wolcott and Lee both devoted long shoots to box suppers, a century-old ritual at one-room schools. With a touch of sadness, however, they also acknowledged that the old ways were quietly slipping away. In the popular book he co-wrote with Walker Evans, *Let Us Now Praise Famous Men* (1941), for example, James Agee condemned Alabama for crowding black children into "stove-heated one-room pine shacks." But he added a barb at the whites' consolidated school, "a recently built, windowy, 'healthfuly' red brick and white-trimmed structure which perfectly exemplifies the American genius for sterility, unimagination, and general gutlessness in meeting any opportunity for 'reform' or 'improvement.'"[12] Even as they struggled to close the one-room school, it seemed, Americans were already mourning its loss.

Sentimentalism, 1930s-Style

The best place to witness this ambivalence was in the cult of the pioneer, which swept an anxious nation in the 1930s. Echoing their Progressive-era forebears, states and communities staged elaborate historical pageants to commemorate their birth and development. Yet pageants in the early 1900s often contained an implicit critique of the present, challenging Americans to remember and even rejuvenate their historic ideals. By contrast, the pageants of the 1930s—like WPA murals and other public art—sought mainly to reassure: despite the many woes of the Depression, history was moving in a positive arc. Even as they celebrated the log-cabin schools of "Old Pioneer Days," then, pageants always concluded with a salute to contemporary education. High schools in New Jersey and Connecticut staged "then and now" dramas on the subject, starting with the little red schoolhouse and ending with the students' own multistoried building. To mark the sesquicentennial of the Northwest Ordinance a national commission sponsored student essay and art contests with the same theme. Winning entries sang the praises of the 1787 Ordinance—which provided for education in new territories—but also stressed growth and improvement since that time. "There were a few rough benches and desks and a stove which was sometimes stubborn and would refuse to heat properly," wrote one ninth-grade essayist from Michigan. "We now have all kinds of schools and everyone has an equal chance for an education."[13]

In fact, the ideal of equality had never been more elusive than it was during the Great Depression. The very need to celebrate progress since pioneer days betrayed a widespread fear of the inverse proposition: that the pioneers embodied basic national virtues that modern-day America had lost. Such worries appear most vividly in children's novels like Carol Ryrie Brink's *Caddie Woodlawn*, winner of the Newbery Medal in 1936. The book tells the story of Brink's grandmother, who had moved with her family from Boston to Wisconsin in the 1850s, and later, after her marriage, to territorial Idaho. As a young girl, Brink had thrilled to her grandmother's tales of hardship and bravery— and, of course, one-room schools—on the frontier. But she also feared that these qualities had disappeared, along with the little red schoolhouse, in the nation's most desperate hour. "If we can just keep hold of some of the sturdy pioneer qualities of these grandparents to hand down to our children, perhaps our children will be better fitted to meet courageously the difficult problems of our modern world," Brink pleaded in her speech accepting the Newbery prize. "It is an entirely different world, but after all the pioneer qualities of courage, willingness to meet the unknown, and steadfastness under difficulties are the things most needed today."[14]

But no pioneer novelist struck a deeper chord during the Depression than Laura Ingalls Wilder, whose *Little House* series detailed her own experiences on the prairie in the 1870s and 1880s. Wilder did not start to write about her life until 1930, when her first effort—an autobiography entitled *Pioneer Girl*—failed to find a publisher. So she turned to historical fiction, embellishing her childhood with archetypal frontier themes. Starting with *On the Banks of Plum Creek* (1937), when Laura and her sister begin their education, the one-room schoolhouse plays a key role in

Wilder's narrative. Poor but proud, Laura survives the teasing of a snobbish "rich girl" at school; in *Little Town on the Prairie* (1941), she must face down an incompetent teacher. Barely older than Laura herself, "Miss Wilder"—the sister of Laura's future husband—cannot control the class; even worse, she unfairly blames Laura for causing disruptions. So the school board replaces her with a man, who quickly whips a troublemaker as an example for the rest. He also prepares Laura and a friend for the end-of-year exhibition, instructing them to recite "the whole of American history, from memory." Laura's friend takes the recent presidents, from John Quincy Adams to Rutherford B. Hayes; Laura is left with the earlier leaders plus all the "discoveries" and "battles," including war on the Indian frontier. She ends her recital with the opening of the trans-Mississippi West, symbolizing the taming of wilderness (and Native Americans) by white families like her own.[15]

Yet Wilder also evinced ambivalence about this so-called civilizing process, especially in *These Happy Golden Years* (1943). Here we find the fifteen-year-old Laura teaching in a one-room school of her own, where sunshine streams through cracks in the wall and a square of painted wood serves as the blackboard. Like her own teacher, she struggles to discipline the "big boys"; like her own father, meanwhile, she fights against the impulse to abandon the very civilization that school represents. "Laura knew just how he felt for she saw the look in his blue eyes as he gazed over the rolling prairie westward," Wilder wrote. "He must stay in a settled country for the sake of them all, just as she must teach school again, though she did so hate to be shut into a schoolroom." So her father helps build a new one-room school, "bright and shining," where Laura is hired to teach. Even in this clean new environment, however, Laura still craves a wild, untamed life: "She wanted to travel on and on, over those miles, and see what lay beyond the hills." Instead, Laura resolves the opposite: "She must be content to stay where she was, to help with the work at home and teach school." Even as it reflected the hard work and self-reliance of the pioneer, in short, the school also symbolized the new constraints of modernity. For every happy step they took toward progress, it seemed, Americans looked back in regret.[16]

Or they simply looked to the last living remnants of real rural simplicity: the Amish of Pennsylvania. As FSA photographs documented, thousands of rural Americans still lived without electricity, running water, and the other conveniences of contemporary life. But the Amish had developed a near-cult following in the popular press by the late 1930s because they *renounced* modernity—including, of course, the modern school. The *New York Times* published no fewer than twenty-three articles over a single year on efforts by Amish parents in East Lampeter, Pennsylvania, to protect their one-room schools from consolidation; even more remarkable, the *Times* routinely referred to these gray-and-white structures as "little red schoolhouses." So did the slew of Amish-related articles and picture books that appeared during these years, transforming a formerly obscure or even threatening people into an icon of pure Americana. The WPA commissioned the artist Katherine Milhous to create a poster of Amish life, which she pointedly entitled "The Little Red Schoolhouse"; a children's book, *Little Amish Schoolhouse* (1939), depicted a red one-room school on its title page; *Travel* magazine entitled its 1940 Amish picture "Lunchtime at the Little Red School-house"; and a 1941 *House and Garden* story on the Amish carried nine school-related photos, including a full-page black-and-white shot of four boys doing sums at the blackboard. In Amish country, the caption said, "home-cropped heads wrestle with the three R's . . . in little red schoolhouses."[17]

Even among professional educators, the one-room school enjoyed a small burst of sentimental popularity. The best example was the famed experimental public elementary school in New York City founded in 1922 that was later dubbed "the Little Red Schoolhouse." Located in Greenwich Village, a hotbed of cultural radicalism, the school stressed active learning, flexible scheduling, and "the spontaneous interest of the child," as one enthusiast wrote in 1930. Like its namesake of old, a second advocate noted, the school also stressed "the sharing of responsibilities in order to achieve a common end." Whereas rural one-room schools mixed different age groups, however, this urban experiment was restricted to a handful of first-graders. But parents, especially those in the immigrant wards, rejected the school's "communal" values. "We send our children to school for what we cannot give them ourselves, grammar and drill," one Italian mother explained. "We do not send our children to school for group activity; they get plenty of that in the street." Only "Fifth Avenue" parents endorsed the school's progressive bent, the mother added. After a 1932 report showing that Little Red Schoolhouse children performed worse on reading tests than children with a similar socioeconomic profile in other classrooms, the Board of Education withdrew its support. Well-heeled supporters continued it as a private school on Bleecker Street, where it remains to this day.[18]

For most Americans, indeed, the little red schoolhouse symbolized traditional rather than progressive instruction. Condemning the "happy anarchy of Rousseau" that reigned in some contemporary classrooms, one New Jersey parent called upon educators to revive the three R's—reading, 'riting, and 'rithmetic—of the old single-teacher school. "Many of us feel that a good proportion of so-called project work is just so much 'kindergarten extension,'" he wrote, noting a "shift of the pendulum" back to conventional methods. "Perhaps the little red schoolhouse on the hill has not lost so much of its redness, after all." Business groups in Detroit invoked similar images to fight municipal tax increases, insisting that the old-timers' "little brown school" provided superior education at a sliver of the cost. In Baltimore the redoubtable H. L. Mencken agreed. Whereas children had walked to one-room schools, Mencken wrote, today's students rode "luxurious busses"; while rural children amused themselves with leapfrog and jacks, contemporary schools hired "elegant experts" to teach them tennis, basketball, and even golf; and whereas the single-room school provided drill in the three R's, modern educators had diluted the curriculum into "practical" pabulum. "The girls were taught to make the dresses in Vogue, and to prepare seven-course meals for ten people," Mencken quipped, "and the boys were thoroly instructed in scoutcraft, salesmanship, and parliamentary law."[19]

Finally, folk artists from the 1930s reflected the same ambivalence about modernity—and the same embrace of the rural one-room school—as novelists, journalists, and educators. Consider *Arbor Day*, the classic 1932 painting by the Iowa artist and teacher Grant Wood. Asked by a local school board to memorialize two deceased country schoolteachers, Wood discovered that one of them had planted trees in front of her school. So he drove around the area with a colleague, drinking whiskey all the while, as he searched for a one-room school with a grove of trees that he could use as a model. When he finally found it, the friend recalled, he was "higher than a cat's back," and doused in nostalgia. "Why don't I paint a picture of all the things that are passing," Wood told her, "the one-room school, the belfry, the horse and wagon, the pump, the coal shed, the outhouse, the walking plow, the dirt road?" All these elements appear on the periphery of *Arbor Day;* in the center, meanwhile, a teacher and her students plant a tree. Against the pretentious affluence of urban society, they speak to a simple agrarianism that America has left behind. "Grant Wood was educated and later became a teacher in just such a little school house," wrote one observer in 1935, in praise of *Arbor Day*. "He paints life as he sees it—with Rotarian heartiness and with a twinkle."[20]

Four years later, the Berkshire Museum in Pittsfield, Massachusetts, displayed another one-room-school image with a much less romantic theme. Submitted for a show on the "World of Today," Nahum Tschacbasov's *Little Red Schoolhouse* (1939) showed students in a typical rural configuration, posing in front of their school for a class picture. There was only one new element: the children all wore gas masks. Tschacbasov was a pioneer in the methods of abstract surrealism, which aimed at "penetration into the subterranean level of the psyche," as the Russian émigré painter told an interviewer. But there was nothing buried or veiled about *The Little Red Schoolhouse*, as one art critic wrote; like the other pictures in the Berkshire exhibit, it reflected a "great concern" with "our nightmare times."[21] War clouds were enveloping Europe yet again, raising the specter of mass death; and with fascism on the march, democracy itself seemed in peril. So Americans would invent a new little red schoolhouse, symbolizing not just their old country virtues but also their new global responsibilities. The fate of the world now rested on the United States— and the United States rested on its one-room schools.

War, the Reds, and the Little Red Schoolhouse

More precisely, the nation *used* to rest on them. World War II would bring yet another round of school closings, as more and more potential instructors were diverted into the war effort: in the two years after America entered the conflict, seven thousand one-room schools shut their doors for lack of teachers. The schools that remained were as impoverished—and inadequate—as ever. "There is trouble at the crossroads, right at the door of the little red schoolhouse," one educator warned at a special 1944 White House conference on rural education. More than 60 percent of one-room-school teachers still lacked a college degree, on average they earned less than half the salary of their urban counterparts, the school term was shorter, and so on. "We are justifiably proud of the splendid, modern schools in our cities and towns," President Roosevelt told the conference. "We cannot be proud of the fact that many of our rural schools, particularly during these years of war, have been sadly neglected." It was to be hoped, reported the *New York Times*, that the White House event would focus needed attention on this problem. "The over-romanticized little red schoolhouse still houses a big percentage of our school population," the *Times* editorialized. "It isn't good enough."[22]

Yet during these same years a new romantic yearning for the little red schoolhouse arose, centered not on sturdy individual virtues but on collective values. During the Depression, the cult of the pioneer had celebrated one-room schools for fostering persistence, hard work, and especially self-reliance. With the country at war, however, single-teacher schools came to represent the shared principles that would bind Americans to each other and help vanquish the fascist foe. To a New York school superintendent, speaking at the hundredth anniversary of the city's first "Red School House," the one-room school taught "service of our country and of mankind"; by honoring it citizens would "strengthen our belief and our appreciation of the American way of life." Even advertisers joined in, linking one-room schools to wartime unity—and, of course, to their own products. "Help your neighbor . . . and help your country," declared a 1944 advertisement for Budweiser beer, next to drawings of a young teacher ringing her handbell at a newly erected one-room school. Just as communities of old cooperated to construct the little red schoolhouse, a caption explained, so today Americans were salvaging paper and scrap metal for the war effort. "That readiness to help the folks down the road and the family across the square was the strength of our early America, the foundation for our democracy," the advertisement declared. "Because of it, we have a greater heritage to defend than any other people on Earth."[23]

In these new paeans to the one-room school, indeed, no theme appeared more commonly—or more floridly—than their connection with democracy. Throughout American history, one educator wrote, rural schools had served as "significant social laboratories" for "the origin and testing of democratic procedures." With the rise of "autocratic forces" across the Atlantic, a second observer noted, Americans needed to remind themselves, and the globe, of the legacy of the little red schoolhouse. "Only America's conscience and education—past, present, and future—can save the spirit of freedom in the world," she declared in 1942. Three years later, American newspapers would report that German generals had surrendered at a "little red schoolhouse" in Reims, France, which served as the headquarters for Allied commander Dwight D. Eisenhower. It made no difference that the brick building was actually a technical college, three stories high and half a city block in length. The enemy *had* to lay down its arms in a little red schoolhouse, for reasons that a Cleveland reporter explained. "How typical of democracy as we know it in this country of ours that the final surrender of Germany should take place in a small red brick schoolhouse," he wrote. "For the little red schoolhouse has played a most important part in the growth of this democracy we cherish so fondly and fight so bravely to defend." Indeed, the reporter concluded, "The victory over Germany . . . is one more victory for the little red schoolhouse."[24]

Such rhetoric was repeated with fresh vigor in the late 1940s and early 1950s, when the hot war against fascism was replaced by a Cold War against a new enemy: communism. Once again the growing sentimentalism surrounding the one-room school contrasted sharply to its actual condition. Spurred by the postwar baby boom, which required new, larger facilities, one-room schools closed at a faster pace than ever. Between 1950 and 1955, Illinois shuttered over 4,000 of its 6,800 one-room schools, while New York's nearly 6,000 of the late 1930s decreased to fewer than 400. But the decline in real numbers, along with the rise of global communism, simply increased the ideological burden on the little red schoolhouse. As in World War II, the one-room school came to represent America's global duty to defend freedom and democracy from the totalitarian challenge. Introducing a 1953 set of essays about Laura Ingalls Wilder's *Little House* series, which was enjoying a new burst of popularity, one critic noted that the pioneer characters in the books "would feel deeply the responsibilities their America must now take in a wider world." The books would also help distinguish and defend the nation from its insidious Soviet enemy, as Wilder's daughter, the anti-Communist crusader Rose Wilder Lane, wrote. Zealously promoting the *Little House* series in schools, Lane argued that her mother's message of frontier self-sufficiency would help children resist the "predominant socialist influences" that had infected the "red schoolhouse" of the present.[25]

During these years, indeed, the little red schoolhouse came to signify not just American democracy but also its negative referent: communism itself. A magazine profile of a young Czech refugee exposed his educational indoctrination in the "Little Red Schoolhouse" back home; the phrase also headlined a cartoon of Joseph Stalin plotting anti-American propaganda at a school desk. And when the Soviets opened a school for diplomats' children in Washington, D.C., it was, inevitably, described as a little red schoolhouse. To conservative activists like Rose Wilder Lane, however, American schools were themselves under threat from the Communist menace. In 1949 a Chicago business association met to debate the question "How Red Is the Little Red Schoolhouse?" Four years later, the same question provided the title for an incendiary leaflet by the far-right author E. M. Root. Its cover showed a simian Soviet soldier using a syringe to inject "Organized Communist Propaganda" into a red school. "Make No Mistake About It! The Treason Ring Is out to Make REDS of *YOUR* Children," the pamphlet blared. Many Reds posed as "liberals" or "progressives," Root cautioned, which made them even more dangerous than out-and-out Communists. "The undercover Red . . . can use his fine-pointed needle to insert the Red poison so cleverly that you can hardly follow his motions . . . and the venom will be deadlier than ever."[26]

Ironically, the very liberals whom Root detested also drew upon the little red schoolhouse to highlight threats against America. To these critics, however, the danger lay less in Communist subversion than in the nation's own departure from its democratic ideals. After the Supreme Court antisegregation decision in *Brown v. Board of Education* (1954), the liberal cartoonist L. D. Warren celebrated with a tableau that showed the Court ejecting a sheep—labeled "Segregation"—from a one-room school; inside the building, a child marked "Dixie" cried. "It was against the rule," Warren's caption declared. As white Southerners resisted integration, meanwhile, Warren and other liberals used the one-room-school image to excoriate them. After schools in Virginia and Arkansas closed to prevent blacks from attending, Saint Louis cartoonist Bill Mauldin drew a smoldering, dilapidated one-room school. "What is done in our classrooms today," Mauldin's caption warned, "will be reflected in the successes or failures of civilization tomorrow." Returning to his Mary-and-her-lamb metaphor in another cartoon, Warren blasted segregationists for blocking federal aid to public schools. A lamb marked "Federal School Aid" tries to enter the one-room school, but Mary ("School Integration") grabs its tail: so long as the racial controversy simmered, it seemed, Americans would never achieve consensus on school funding.[27]

Other artists and cartoonists used one-room-school imagery to condemn overcrowded classrooms, a persistent problem in the baby-boom years of the 1950s. In Suffolk County, Long Island, where the school population doubled in five years, many school districts held double or even triple sessions; others rented space in storefronts, firehouses, and churches. In California, communities erected Quonset huts to contain their overflow students; and in Fairfax, Virginia, school officials rented five new homes from a developer and converted them into temporary classrooms. To dramatize these difficulties, one cartoonist depicted a single-room schoolhouse marked "School Construction" in a losing footrace with a stork, which carried away bundles of children. Another showed a student ("Growing Enrollment") kicking his foot through the one-room school as a frustrated schoolteacher rang her handbell in alarm. "He's through as soon as he starts!" the caption complained. The problem of school overcrowding connected directly to federal aid, as a third cartoon made clear. Standing in front of a one-room school marked "Inadequate School Construction Program," President Eisenhower tries to comfort a sad child. "It's not the principle—it's the money," Eisenhower lamely explains.[28]

Whatever their political bent, then, artists and writers imagined the little red schoolhouse as a sacred entity; whether threatened by communism or racism or simple stinginess, the one-room school itself was pure and unspoiled. The rare exceptions to this rule tended to reinforce it. The novelist Henry Roth, a Jewish immigrant, produced two unpublished short stories in the 1940s about one-room schools in Maine, where Roth had moved from New York City. Perhaps inspired by the experiences of Roth's wife, who taught at a local elementary school, both stories depict the school as a cesspool of poverty, bigotry, and ignorance. "Imagine trying to teach seven different grades, 24 kids, all of them with a tradition of neglected schooling and hell-raising," the narrator begins the first story. "Well, I want to tell you— Inadequate teaching material, inadequate play facilities, inadequate everything." The superintendent compounds the narrator's woes by barring him from smoking, which the narrator simply ignores; his cigarette, he says, is his only pleasure of the day. In the next story, two students bait the Jewish narrator with anti-Semitic slurs; he confronts the children's father, who denounces him to the school board as a Communist. But the board stands by him. "On the whole I think I've increased my standing in the community," the narrator concludes. "It was just one of those cases where you had to stand and fight, and if your cause was just, the rotten and the mean were going to be defeated."[29]

In the rare instances where authors or artists set out to attack the one-room school, then, they often reverted to an idyllic image of it. Ostensibly critical, both of Roth's stories end on a positive note: the superintendent looks the other way when the narrator smokes; the school board turns away the prejudiced persecutors. Even John Steinbeck, no friend of the American small town, put in a good word for the one-room school in *East of Eden* (1952). "The country schools were the centers of culture," Steinbeck declared, recalling rural California in the late 1800s. "In the country the repository of art and science was the school, and the schoolteacher shielded and carried the torch of learning and of beauty." Other writers apologized for their romantic paeans to the one-room school, openly acknowledging their distortions of it. By the time she finished her popular children's book *Schoolhouse in the Woods* (1949), the Kentucky novelist Rebecca Caudill told her publicist, she had "a genuine case of nostalgia." True, she quickly added, "educators must be right" about the inadequacies of the little red schoolhouse. "But this moment, with the spell of the woods . . . on me, I'm glad I came up thru a one-room school." Writing from Detroit, where he taught high school, another Kentucky native made a similar confession. "We oldsters know all the advantages of the larger, more impersonal, better equipped consolidated school," wrote Edgar Logan, who had walked a mile each way to his one-room school. "But we can't help looking backward over our shoulders at the warm, cozy, memory tinted school days of yesteryear." Neither could thousands of other Americans, who would devise new and creative means to remember them.[30]

Rituals of Loss and Memory

Across the country, the most popular way to commemorate the one-room school was to gather there when it closed. Schools held reunion picnics or dinners on their final day, attracting old-timers as well as present-day students. In search of their former desks and benches, alumni scanned the jackknifed initials that still decorated much of the school's interior, while bleary-eyed children posed outside the building to wave good-bye to their teacher, in a scene often captured by local newspapers. Even a 1956 groundbreaking ceremony for a consolidated school in rural Pennsylvania heard poetic testimonies to a nearby one-room school, which had shut down the previous year:

Little schoolhouse on the hill
Toll your bell, time stands not still
Bless you as we close your door
And bless the days that come no more
. . . .

Outside "bathrooms," draft, chill
And belly-flopping down the hill
Hiking in the woods in spring
Wonderment in everything

. . . .

Living learning every day
From harvest time to merry May
Little school, your work is done
Ring your bell for laurels won.[31]

In a more commercial vein, local districts also staged auctions when closing their one-room schools. Saying farewell to the school, residents bid small sums on desks, bells, books, stoves, and swings. Wealthier citizens occasionally bought the entire school, which they might convert into a full-time residence or a summer home; other schools became sheds, grain bins, garages, offices, or roadside cafés. Newspapers carried advertisements for "School House and Supplies" auctions, which drew crowds from near and far. "The little red schoolhouse is for sale," one paper reported. "Matter-of-fact buyers and sentimental onlookers trail the auctioneer from district to district to witness the finish of a famous American institution." Magazines and newspapers also ran advertisements for school furniture, which found its way from auctions and dealers to department stores. In New York, Macy's offered an original teacher's desk and stool, priced at $89.95; for $149, buyers could purchase a set of six two-seat "twin" student desks. "Come see these treasures we've scouted out, tinkered with, polished up into useful and delightful furniture for today's homes," Macy's urged.[32]

Other businesses sought to capitalize on the image of the little red schoolhouse, which became ever more evocative as actual one-room schools disappeared. A resort in the Catskill Mountains of New York offered a day camp for children in its "New Little Red Schoolhouse"; a toy manufacturer sold Little Red Schoolhouse bricks, which could be assembled to form a one-room school; one department store marketed a back-to-school bag to young girls that featured a red schoolhouse on the front; and another sold a wooden clock shaped like a one-room school, complete with a brass bell. The most elaborate commercial tribute to the institution appeared in a Parker Brothers board game, released in 1952. Echoing the quiz-show craze of the 1950s, the Little Red School House Game challenged players with history and geography questions ("Who painted the Mona Lisa?" "What is the chief crop of China?") or "mental arithmetic" puzzlers: like students of old, contestants would have to calculate sums and fractions in their heads. Each question appeared on a card that bore a drawing of a red schoolhouse, marked "District 2," with three windows on each side, a schoolmarm ringing a bell in the doorway, and children milling around in the yard. The same drawing decorated the boxtop, which Parker Brothers advertised alongside Monopoly, Clue, and its other products.[33]

Finally, communities began efforts to preserve one-room schools as "living museums" and shrines to their educational past. Residents in Woodstock, Connecticut, rallied to save their old schoolhouse, which had served the town continuously from 1748 to 1943. Working through their congressman, they won a letter of support from President Harry Truman; two years later, when the restored school was dedicated, a congratulatory statement was read from Truman's successor, Dwight D. Eisenhower. "This should be an occasion for rededication to the idea that an educated citizenry is a primary requisite for our form of government," Eisenhower declared, echoing the Cold War theme of democracy in a dangerous world. But local citizens seemed more interested in the everyday customs and rituals of the one-room school than in its implications for international affairs. Gathering outside the school in Civil War–era costume, they rushed inside to admire the lunch pails, water bucket, and dunce cap; while next to the teacher's desk they inspected a switch cut from a nearby elm tree. Former instructors played an especially prominent role in these projects. In Oberlin, Ohio, a local teacher contributed her own handbell and rocking chair to a restored 1836 school, and when the old schoolhouse in New Canaan, Connecticut, reopened for visitors, its last teacher stood in the doorway, bell in hand, to greet the first guests.[34]

The best-known restored schools were the seven buildings that Henry Ford refurbished or built for his Greenfield Village historical park in Dearborn, Michigan, which drew a million tourists a year by the end of the 1950s. Two of the schools had been attended by Ford himself; another was William Holmes McGuffey's childhood home, which Ford purchased and moved from western Pennsylvania. The schools were among the most popular destinations at the village, especially after NBC's *Today Show* and *Howdy Doody Show* staged segments of pupils studying there in 1955. By this time Greenfield Village had segregated students by age; for example, only sixth-graders attended Scotch Settlement, Ford's first boyhood school. To give the school a more "old-fashioned" feel, NBC brought in pupils of varied ages from the other village schools. It also paid actors to perform as students and even as the teacher, who was coached by the school's actual instructor. "The children and I had fun practicing for the show," the real teacher recalled, "although we were seen for only a few minutes."[35]

To widen the audience for his collection of memorabilia, Ford also sponsored several traveling exhibits: *Main Street USA, Industrial Progress USA*, and *Schoolroom Progress USA*. Moving about the country on railroad cars, these exhibits linked past and present into an unbroken chain: proudly displaying early technologies, they also underscored subsequent advances and the overall positive arc of history itself. "See the OLD and the NEW," declared an announcement for the school exhibit, which was free and open to the public for five years. It began with a log-cabin school, complete with oil lamps, backless benches, quill pens, a dunce cap, and a birch switch. Then it moved on to "the famous 'little red schoolhouse,'" featuring twin desks, slates, and a stove. Next came a "Gay Ninetees" urban schoolroom, with cast-iron furniture and "Thomas Edison's amazing new electric light." The exhibit concluded with a contemporary classroom, leaving little doubt about its overall superiority. "You'll see what's new today—the latest in educational facilities—startling, modern schoolrooms designed by America's foremost architects," promoters boasted. "Bring the whole family to this amazing exhibit of America's educational past, present, and future."[36]

Around the country, however, observers rejected this optimistic message of progress and improvement; for many Americans, indeed, memories of the one-room school highlighted national decline more than national development. "The pictures in your article brought back many pleasant recollections of my early youth," wrote one suburban New Yorker, thanking a newspaper for a photo essay about his own one-room school. "In the 'little red' schoolhouses the boys and girls of our country learned not only the three R's, but were also inculcated [with] a strict moral code, proper courtesy to others and good personal behavior." Such critics focused especially upon the much-reported waves of juvenile delinquency in American cities, which seemed to underscore the nation's neglect of its old rural virtues. They also targeted progressive education, a favorite scapegoat of Cold War conservatives; to these "old fogies," one wag wrote, modern schools had replaced fundamental skills with a feeble menu of vocational choices. "They believe that real pumpkin pie and restaurant clam chowder are different than 50 years ago," he quipped. "They may also have the notion that spellers are not comparable to the good old days." From East Africa an American missionary added a third note of regret: whereas the one-room school taught religion, modern public schools had removed it. "In America there is not freedom enough to read God's Word and pray within the confines of the little red schoolhouse," he wrote.[37]

As in the Progressive era itself, handfuls of Americans remembered one-room schools as the embodiment of progressive education. In 1955, for example, the *New York Daily News* published a flattering article about the "Little Red Schoolhouse" in the Bronx, one of the city's only former one-room schools that remained in operation. It now had three classrooms, combining two grades in each room. "New York's most progressive educational practices are followed in this old fashioned school," the article gushed. In age-mixed classrooms, the *News* reported, children taught one another; and all of them knew their teachers, who resided in the same community. An accompanying photograph showed the school's old bell, which had been brought down from the belfry and mounted in the foyer. Now it rang only "when mischief gets the better of little boys," the caption read. In the picture, a boy rings the bell while a girl holds her ears; as the girl confirmed many years later in her own article about the little red schoolhouse, the entire photo was staged. Nevertheless, she too remembered the picture, and her school, with affection and admiration. In the 1960s, especially, citizens of every type would find their own reasons to love the little red schoolhouse.[38]

Open Classroom or Back to Basics?

In 1974 education professor Halas Jackim spearheaded a campaign to restore an abandoned one-room schoolhouse at the State University of New York, Oswego. Jackim had recently helped found the One Room School House Association, which located and purchased the school; now he needed funds to move the old building to his campus, where it would remind students and other visitors about the historical roots of "progressive" teaching methods. "This project will bring into focus the fact that many of the 'new' ideas in education, such as the open classroom and the ungraded school, were ideas used in the one-room schoolhouses," Jackim declared. After the restored school reopened, Jackim's students mimicked this perspective almost word for word. "Today the 'new' systems of modern education are reverting back to the teaching techniques of the one-room schoolhouse: the open classroom and nongraded classes," one student wrote in her term paper. In the margin, Professor Jackim signaled his approval: "Good point."[1]

Off campus, however, many Oswego citizens didn't get it. To one resident, writing anonymously in the local newspaper, the restored schoolhouse would teach the community about *traditional* values—patriotism, faith, and discipline—rather than "progressive" ones. At the one-room school the writer attended, each day began with the Pledge of Allegiance and the Lord's Prayer. "We loved our country and obeyed its laws; we respected our flag, our school, each other, and ourselves! There was no painting on the walls, no destroying property that didn't belong to us." The school focused squarely on the three R's, eschewing frills like art or gym; and sex education was provided not by the teacher but by parents, "when we were old enough." Most of all, children obeyed adult authority. "We knew to appreciate our parents, respect our elders, and our country," the writer recalled. "Let us not forget!" Lest anyone miss the point, finally, the writer signed the letter in capitals: "JUST AN OLD FASHIONED AMERICAN, AND DARN GLAD OF IT." Once the school was restored, the writer added, it should be painted in red, white, and blue.[2]

These differing reactions underscore the divisions and distortions surrounding the little red schoolhouse from the 1960s into the present. Liberal Americans imagined the one-room school as the lodestar of open education and other cutting-edge pedagogies, turning a blind eye to the poverty, violence, and harsh discipline that marked many single-teacher schools. Meanwhile, conservatives supposed that the school was more disciplined—and more effective—than it really was: contrary to the claims of Oswego's "Old Fashioned American," for example, students carved up their desks and chairs with as much zeal as any latter-day graffiti artist. But both sides joined hands around the *image* of the little red schoolhouse, manipulating it for their own political purposes. In 1965, for example, Lyndon Johnson returned to his old one-room school in Texas—long since converted into a private home—to sign the Elementary and Secondary Education Act. He also flew in his former teacher, "Miss Kate," amusing the audience with stories of reciting his first lessons on her lap. Even Johnson's wife described the setting as "corny" for the signing of "a great education bill" that would forever alter the traditional local governance of American schools. In his own speech, meanwhile, the president linked the one-room school to his major domestic initiative: the War on Poverty. "As the son of a tenant farmer, I know that education is the only valid passport from poverty," he declared.[3]

Like the one-room school in Oswego, Johnson's former school would soon become a tourist site. With so many Americans invoking the symbolism of the little red schoolhouse—and with so few one-room schools still in operation—schoolhouse preservation and tourism boomed. By 1982, Kansas alone had opened nine restored one-room schools to visitors; two decades later New York State would boast over eighty such projects. The restoration of an old school often highlighted present-day political differences in a community, as the Oswego case illustrates. But it could also bring citizens together, galvanizing them around a shared emblem from the past. After Johnson's one-room-school ceremony, a New Jerseyan wrote the president to plead for assistance in preserving his own one-room schoolhouse. "To those people who grew up in this community the closing of the schoolhouse will be sad," he wrote. "It belonged to the days when life was a little more secure, the days when a farm meant hard work but plenty of good living." Indeed, a Michigan preservationist added, it was hard to imagine the rural community without its one-room school. "Is there no way to preserve the good from the past when we go on to the new?" he asked. "Must the fine community spirit—the togetherness—go with the building?"[4]

By the 1990s, these sentiments would coalesce into a new bipartisan demand for smaller schools—and a new historical embrace of the little red schoolhouse. Nearly two thousand preservation projects sprouted up around the country, often focused explicitly on the snug, communal aspects of the one-room school. In Maine, where ten schools were restored, one teacher brought her class to visit an old school and came away with a new commitment to "collaboration and cooperation" in her own classroom. Hence the title of her recollections, "Circling Back," which called upon contemporary educators to recapture the intimate, face-to-face bonds of the single-teacher school. The same impulse underlay urban efforts to create charter schools and other smaller alternatives to the large, alienating modern school. Boston's Bruce Hammond caught the irony of this trend in a 1997 cartoon, which—like the Maine teacher's memoirs—drew on the metaphor of the circle. A bus marked "education" travels around a city, then doubles back to the one-room school where it began. "Well, we've certainly come a long way," the caption declared. Looking to repair their broken schools, Americans again looked backward to the little red schoolhouse.[5]

Showdown at the Little Red Schoolhouse: Education and Memory in the 1960s and 1970s

In 1964 the top-rated local half-hour television show in the northeastern United States featured a miniature red building with a slanted roof and a small blackboard. The show had a predictable title—*The Little Red Schoolhouse*—with a customary motif: a "schoolmaster" posed questions to students, who assembled in panels of four in front of the "school." Advertisements for the program drew on equally familiar themes, depicting its name in childlike block letters and warning that the schoolbell would soon ring on the final episode. *The Little Red Schoolhouse* had begun as a radio show in 1938, shifting to television in 1940, but it was dropped when audiences failed to tune in. The quiz shows of the 1950s (and their related scandals) brought more viewers aboard, spawning a revival of the program in 1963. Like its predecessors, *The Little Red Schoolhouse* fused old-fashioned rote pedagogy—questions and answers—with modern media technology. "A Battle of Brains," promised one advertisement. "Join us for this exciting new quiz show that puts the emphasis on knowledge and quick recall."[6]

To a new generation of educators, however, schooling meant more than mere memorization and recitation at the feet of a stern taskmaster. Streaming from college campuses into new teaching positions, these left-leaning Americans conceived of education as child-centered, activity-based, and social: rather than seeking to inscribe the proverbial right answer on each individual, education should engage students' natural curiosity in a collective quest for truth. Such critics took special aim at age-segregated grades, which took no account of children's diverse abilities and interests. So they seized on the little red schoolhouse, too, but for a new reason: rather than embodying the dull rhythms of rote, it symbolized the lively mixing of ages. Whereas the one-room school combined different students, one educator explained, "too many of us continue to place them in lock-step, graded school organizations that assume that all children . . . are ready to absorb a given instructional diet at the same rate." More than 10 percent of urban elementary schools had established mixed-age classes by 1968, often drawing on rural one-room schools as a precedent. "Grandmother and her teacher might get a chuckle out of some of the 'educational jargon' used to describe procedures and methods which were perfectly familiar to them in their village school," one observer wrote, praising a mixed-age classroom. "As we all know, with many grades taught in one classroom, each student was forced to help another."[7]

Indeed, educators said, the one-room school pioneered another part of their progressive philosophy: group learning. Whatever their ages, this doctrine held, students learned better from one another than they did from adults. "In education, maybe we need to rediscover the wheel," remarked California school superintendent Wilson Riles, who had taught in a one-room school early in his career. "People need to learn from one another, no matter how different they are." Most of all, students discovered that education was a shared responsibility: even as they developed individual skills, they learned to care for their peers. "In that richly varied one-room community there was no artificial separation of children into good and bad, smart and dumb, young and old," one memoirist wrote. "We were all in it together." The group-instruction movement spawned a host of news reports about America's last remaining one-room schools, where the virtues of the technique were still on display. Serving as an aide in a Vermont school, one Middlebury College student found nothing less than an educational utopia: children all learned at their own pace, but each one contributed something vital to the class as a whole. "The one-room school may be old fashioned, but it is in no way backward," he wrote. "Some so-called modern schools might well benefit from taking a closer look."[8]

Other left-leaning educators invoked one-room schools on behalf of the "open" school, perhaps the most modern—and the most controversial—innovation of all. Open schools removed classroom walls and substituted portable partitions, creating a wide variety of shared settings—and inevitable comparisons to the little red schoolhouse. One new school in California "called back to life the one-room school concept," as an enthusiast wrote, creating "two large one-room schoolhouses" that were each the size of five standard classrooms; by removing the bulletin boards between them, teachers could even convert the school into a single huge space. Between 1966 and 1969, when one new school per day was built in California, 20 percent of new elementary buildings had completely open interiors; by 1972, a single county in Colorado had erected fifteen "schools without walls." Like group learning, the trend sent news reporters streaming back into America's remaining one-room schools. Quoting an instructor at one of Vermont's nine single-teacher schools, a newspaper described the open school as "just another name" for the one-room school; to illustrate an article about a one-room school in Montana, meanwhile, another paper printed a photograph with a caption that read, simply, "Open Classroom."[9]

At the most radical end of the educational spectrum, finally, still other Americans linked the rural one-room school to urban calls for community control. Across the country, largely African American activists demanded the power to select curricula and staff in schools; in New York's Ocean Hill–Brownsville district, most famously, their efforts triggered a citywide teachers strike. Establishing a nongraded elementary school, Ocean Hill leaders deemed it "as old as the one-room rural schoolhouse"; even more, they said, the plea for community control echoed the local rule of the little red schoolhouse. "We want our sisters and brothers to teach our children for eight years," one black parent in Chicago explained. "Our great grandparents with extremely limited education taught in one room schools . . . so we know that we can teach our own." More than anything else, another Illinois observer noted, the clamor for community control reflected public impatience with present-day educational bureaucracies. No wonder so many Americans now looked back fondly at the one-room school, uniting "nostalgic oldtimers and sophisticated radicals alike," as the historian David Tyack wrote in 1972. Whatever their politics, it seemed, all could find something to like in the little red schoolhouse.[10]

On the right, meanwhile, "nostalgic oldtimers" enlisted the single-teacher school behind *their* favored values: order, authority, and faith. Most liberal one-room-school enthusiasts were too young to have attended such an institution themselves and were forced to draw on others' accounts to imagine it. But conservatives often had direct experience of the little red schoolhouse, which they invoked against the protest and chaos of the late 1960s and early 1970s. "We learned discipline at school and at home," one Kentucky citizen recalled, in a typical passage. "We were taught to respect our teachers and obey them," another added. Even the one-room school's much-maligned system of rote learning instilled discipline in children, as a former Iowa teacher remembered. "Hearing 24 classmates recite a table individually may be boring," she wrote, "but knowing your turn will come . . . can be an incentive to concentrate." For students who got out of line, finally, a stern whipping would bring them back in. After one boy threw mud balls, another former teacher from Iowa wrote, she made him cut a switch from the woods and then applied it to his bottom. "It is difficult to evaluate or measure character building," she admitted, "but I like to think that [I] helped the pupil to become a more worthwhile, honorable citizen of the United States."[11]

Another source of character in the little red schoolhouse was spiritual instruction, especially via prayer and Bible reading. To conservatives' chagrin, however, religion, like corporal punishment, had largely disappeared from contemporary schools. "The well-known 'three Rs' (now representing reading and 'riting and 'rithmetic) was originally reading and 'riting and *religion*," underlined one author in a 1972 tribute to the one-room school. "It does seem a pity, or even a disgrace, that the Bible, which began American education and taught so many lessons of morality just as important as arithmetic, should now be banned from most of our schooling. It is, in my mind, bigotry in reverse." A similar indignation marked other right-wing memoirs of the little red schoolhouse, especially with regard to holiday services. "Do you remember when it wasn't a federal offense to have a Christmas program in a public school?" a former teacher wrote. Even worse, another critic added, present-day schools had substituted sex education for the spiritual kind. "I learned the 'bad words' and the birds and the bees from the printed, written, and carved words found on the backside of the schoolhouse," he wrote. "I do not consider all this sex education and modernistic education doings to be extremely necessary."[12]

All these themes—faith, discipline, and the rejection of "modernistic" schools—came together in a remarkable 1975 comic book by Al Hartley, who produced Christian-themed "Archie" comics for the religious publisher Fleming H. Revell. Entitled "Showdown at the Little Red Schoolhouse," the comic depicts its freckled hero, Archie Andrews, as a sheriff in the Old West. Archie's friend Jughead is cast as "Pronto," his "faithful Indian companion," who bursts into the local saloon in search of Archie. (Our hero is drinking a milkshake, not alcohol, drawing hoots from other patrons.) "The School Marm needs you right away!!!" Pronto announces breathlessly. "They've got heap big trouble at the school!!!" Sheriff Archie rides his white stallion to the little red schoolhouse, where the School Marm (played by Betty, his erstwhile love interest) is waiting by the fence. "When they took the Bible out of school, more and more problems came in," she tells Archie. "Now we have books that say we all came from monkeys, and the students are starting to act like it!" Here the School Marm points to the little red schoolhouse, which emits clouds and stars of noise and disruption. "Our young people deserve better than this," the School Marm sighs, holding a book called *Evolution Is for the Birds and You*. But Sheriff Archie saves the day. He prevails upon a rich banker to pay for new books, which Archie unloads (from a wagon marked "Fleming H. Revell Co.") at a Christian bookstore.[13]

The Archie comic drew on popular imagery in postwar film and television westerns as well as on children's books like Laura Ingalls Wilder's *Little House* series, which experienced yet another burst of popularity in the 1960s and 1970s. The Wilder books also spawned a successful television show (*Little House on the Prairie*, 1974–83) starring Michael Landon, who had made his acting name in the western television hit *Bonanza*. Whereas traditional westerns often celebrated the lone outlaw, however, Landon's *Little House* series, like its 1970s competitor, *The Waltons*, emphasized the shared burdens and triumphs of a hardscrabble family. The product of an unhappy marriage, Landon depicted the type of close-knit family he had always sought but never found in his own youth. To be sure, several new themes marked the western and its ubiquitous schoolmarm. In the hit musical film *Cat Ballou* (1965), for example, a prim teacher (played by Jane Fonda) straps on six-shooters to avenge her father's death; in the television series *Sara* (1976) the title character travels West on her own to teach in a one-room school. Despite these nods to contemporary feminism, however, the western served mainly to reinforce traditional gender roles. In the Audie Murphy blockbuster *The Quick Gun* (1964), for example, a lone male hero vanquishes his foes and reunites with "his" one-room-school marm, who had waited patiently for him to return.[14]

For conservatives, stunned by youth rebellions and rising divorce rates, the modern western expressed a longing for the stable, two-parent American family. It could also reflect an animus against civil rights and racial integration, as the Archie comic further illustrates. As if evolution instruction and the removal of the Bible were not bad enough, Pronto tells Sheriff Archie, the little red schoolhouse was forced to accept new students from outside the community. "They've had their hands full ever since they started to bus students across the prairie!" Pronto exclaims, riding by a wagon marked "School Bus." Indeed, as courts issued school desegregation orders, the busing issue galvanized white conservatives around their own brand of community control. To urban blacks, the term denoted efforts to wrest impoverished districts from white-led city school boards; but to white suburbanites, it referred to their own campaigns against "forced busing" with African Americans. Like their militant black counterparts, right-wing whites would also enlist the image of the one-room school. In 1972, for example, a thirty-three-hundred-car motorcade of white parents from the Richmond, Virginia, area converged on Washington, D.C., to protest a court desegregation decree. Backing up traffic outside the capital for twenty-five miles, each car in the motorcade bore the insignia of a little red schoolhouse.[15]

The anti-busing movement sparked a new round of debate about the one-room school, featuring the usual mix of polemics and parody. "All of this talk about the evils of busing is almost amusing," wrote John Hope Franklin, a leading African American historian. "Back in the 1930s and 1940s children all over the country, especially in rural areas, were bused to new centralized schools. No one ever complained." Here Franklin distorted for effect: thousands of rural parents *did* resist consolidation, struggling to retain their single-teacher schools. Other liberal critics acknowledged as much but went on to argue that these parents were simply wrong: as one law professor wrote, one-room schools could not provide the "educational benefits" of their consolidated counterparts. Looking back on his own youth, an Iowan admitted that his parents had resisted the "forced integration" of his one-room school into a larger metropolitan system; like contemporary conservatives, they feared long bus rides and "different kinds of peoples and cultures." But they were wrong, too. Thanks to consolidation, he had developed "a broader outlook on life" than the one-room school could offer. So would present-day anti-busing activists, if they could only temper their romantic attachment to all-white schools.[16]

Even among left-leaning Americans, however, the negative image of the little red schoolhouse as narrow, parochial, and prejudiced had little appeal. As one Kentucky journalist noted, people who had actually attended a one-room school frequently forgot its less savory aspects. Whatever their personal history or politics, moreover, citizens tended to associate the one-room school with a disappearing feature of modern life: interaction with the local community. As shopping malls and superhighways enveloped their old stores and streets, Americans of every stripe joined hands to preserve abandoned schools. "Children should know that life here has not always been housing developments and ice cream carts," explained a member of a new historical society in Madison, New Jersey, forged to restore its one-room school. "The little building will stand as a reminder of the days before it was swallowed by the suburbs." Meanwhile, nearby Lyndhurst kept its one-room school open by assigning first-graders to it. "We maintain it for sentimental reasons," an official admitted. "It's just like a national monument, like the Liberty Bell. It gives us a feeling of being, of purpose."[17]

To anxious Americans, indeed, the one-room school symbolized not just their vanishing local communities but the enduring nation that bound them together. By the Bicentennial celebration of 1976, hundreds of towns and villages had begun efforts to preserve their one-room schools. Some of these campaigns were spearheaded by local historical societies, others by area universities, and still others by private citizens. Two teenaged brothers in South Dakota sold their 4-H calves to purchase their former school, which had been vandalized by arsonists; they moved it to the state fairgrounds, where other volunteers restored and prepared it for visitors. Other local groups received restoration grants from the America the Beautiful Fund, begun a decade earlier at Lady Bird Johnson's White House Conference on Natural Beauty to sponsor "citizen-initiated volunteer activities." One-room schoolhouses became a favorite target for the fund's largesse precisely because so many people were interested in them. "They are part of a growing grass-roots movement—plain citizens who are salvaging the history of America before it falls down, is paved over, or dies with the last memories," explained one grant recipient.[18]

Most of all, preservation efforts were championed by former teachers—especially veterans of the one-room school. To commemorate the Bicentennial, the National Retired Teachers Association urged each state chapter to prepare a book about the "early experiences of teachers" and "the types of educational institutions of the past." Single-room teachers and schools figured largely in these accounts, sparking a new awareness of abandoned schools and a new resolve to restore them. In Iowa, where more than two thousand of the state's ten thousand one-room schools were still standing, one former teacher wrote a poem to encourage their preservation. "The old stone school still stands / On the knoll at the bend in the road," the poem began, in a nod to John Greenleaf Whittier's famous verse. It went on to describe the decay of the building, then concluded on a plaintive note: "Will a century of history be forgotten / That should be preserved for posterity?" In Ohio, meanwhile, an ex-teacher introduced a bill in the state legislature to fund a restored one-room school at his alma mater, Bowling Green. "There is a strong educational tie between the little red schoolhouse and the big university," Bowling Green's president declared. Indeed, another spokesman added, the preserved school would help "close the generation gap" on campus. "Old-timers can have a nostalgic touch," he explained, "and today's 'mods' can see what their grandparents have been talking about."[19]

Retired teachers also played a key role in living history reenactments at restored one-room schools, which began in the late 1960s and picked up steam around the Bicentennial. Student and youth groups would visit for the day to experience the school "as it really was": they recited from McGuffey's, wrote on slates, and donned the dunce cap when the teacher so dictated. Dressed in a hoop skirt with bell in hand, this "School Marm" was frequently a former teacher; in rare instances, she had actually taught in the school herself. These programs drew accolades from older adults, who got a chance to re-create their own youth, but decidedly mixed receptions from visiting children. Some students objected to sharing space with different age groups, others to hauling wood for the stove, and still others to the absence of television and radio. Most of all young visitors condemned the tedious recitations and the strict discipline that enforced them. "After seeing that stick they used to punish the bad kids, I'm glad I'm going to school today, instead of then," said one ten-year-old at the Sterling School in Sudbury, Massachusetts, that Henry Ford had restored many years before. In the 1980s champions of the little red schoolhouse would seek to revive precisely the qualities this boy rejected: discipline and the three R's. Calling their campaign "Back to Basics," they too looked back to the one-room school.[20]

The 1980s and 1990s: Back to Basics?

In 1980 the National Endowment of the Humanities awarded a team of scholars $260,0000 to document America's vanishing rural schools. Over the next two years, the "Country School Legacy" project sent 23 researchers into eight states to locate old schools, sift through archives, and conduct interviews. To elicit citizen input, meanwhile, the project also sponsored more than 250 public seminars. In their internal memoranda, seminar leaders warned against distorting the little red schoolhouse: rather than simply singing the praises of the one-room school, seminars should promote critical reflection about it. As they soon discovered, however, this was easier said than done. "After two sessions, it seems that *nobody* wants to talk about any of the weaknesses or problems facing country schools, so to run an unbiased discussion is a tough task," underlined one seminar leader from Chadron, Nebraska. "I'm not about to attack country schools in western Nebraska (it could be fatal), but I do get a bit concerned about the reluctance to deal with issues." Whenever she raised the drawbacks of the one-room school—poor facilities, inadequate instruction, limited curricula—audiences bridled. They focused instead on its virtues, especially its emphasis on reading, writing, and arithmetic. "The cry," another seminar leader wrote, "is Back to Basics."[21]

Capitalized for good measure, Back to Basics first appeared as a rallying call in the mid-1970s. Amid reports of declining test scores and lax classroom discipline, thirty-eight states passed laws requiring public schools to administer so-called minimum competency examinations. The movement picked up steam with the conservative resurgence of 1980, which brought Ronald Reagan into the White House. As governor of California, Reagan had criticized low academic standards, warning that "schools are not playgrounds." But the jeremiad became louder with his ascension to the presidency and the release of *A Nation at Risk* (1983), a federal report that blamed American schools for the country's feeble economic performance. At the same time, the right-wing revival spawned a new skepticism about government taxation and spending. Even as they condemned schools for failing to teach the three R's, conservatives pointed out that educational costs continued to skyrocket. So they turned naturally to the one-room schoolhouse, which allegedly delivered a superior product at a sliver of the price. "The little red schoolhouse worked," declared the columnist Patrick Buchanan, who served as Reagan's communications director. "Today, schools that spend 20 times per capita what these schools did, fail."[22]

To Back to Basics enthusiasts, the cost and mission of one-room schools were closely linked: precisely *because* the schools were so poor in money and equipment, they had little choice but to focus on basic literacy and numeracy. Conservatives even defended the bête noire of liberal educators, rote instruction, which transmitted broader lessons about persistence, obedience, and discipline. "You didn't spell a word or pronounce it correctly once and end it there—you came back to it," one memoirist wrote. "You learned that the way to study involved going over the important things again and again." Students had learned the now-lost art of handwriting via the Palmer method, drawing endless rows of ovals in their copybooks; they had also memorized poetry and geography, reciting Whittier and Longfellow along with the names of rivers, mountains, and national capitals. Most of all, they had learned the value of work itself. In a much-quoted 1981 interview, the psychologist Bruno Bettelheim praised the one-room school as "the best school we ever had" because it required labor, attention, and effort from all the students. By contrast, present-day schools let them slide. "Everything gets equal praise from the teacher," Bettelheim complained. "The worst aspect of the system is that we try to make education easier and easier. To become educated isn't easy."[23]

The one-room-school teacher could demand obedience and hard work from her students, Bettelheim added, because they shared a "common background"; not so in contemporary classrooms, where they often came from different worlds. Indeed, other conservatives admitted, the order and discipline of the little red schoolhouse rested on its racial and economic homogeneity. "Perhaps it is easier to know what you want out of your school if the parent group has much in common—such as ethnic background, cultural background, financial standing, similar work," several Wyoming citizens observed. "The transitory population is now so mixed in morals, requirements of our children, and of each other that we do not all think in the same direction." As in the 1970s, some conservatives condemned forced busing for eroding the community spirit—and the all-white constituency—of one-room schools. Others acknowledged the old schools' ethnic diversity but insisted that they had treated everybody the same. "There were many different nationalities and religious backgrounds, but . . . I never was aware that there was the slightest difference in any of us," one Michigan resident recalled. With the rise of multicultural education, however, schools needlessly accented racial diversity. "Today," another Michiganite quipped, "the 3 R's in schools are Recycling, Racism, and Reproduction."[24]

The last *R* referred to sex education, of course, which symbolized the decline of traditional morality, not just traditional pedagogy, in American schools. At the one-room school she attended in rural Ohio, one woman recalled, girls dressed and behaved with modesty. "Clothing was strictly to cover our bodies," she wrote. "Style never seemed to bother us, nothing to encourage youthful romance, surely!" True, as Mark Twain's stories illustrated, boys and girls flirted and courted: they shared lunches, passed messages, and became secretly "engaged." But these innocent dalliances also rested on a shared moral code of reticence, conservatives said, which had melted away in the hypersexualized heat of modernity. In the era of the little red schoolhouse, the argument went, school and home had reinforced each other. Yet today's families were failing to impart essential moral lessons, as witness the rise in teen pregnancy, violence, and drug use, and schools were powerless to pick up the slack. New laws and regulations prohibited corporal punishment, which had taught one-room-school children "the difference between right and wrong," as one observer recalled. ("Perhaps if there were a little less sparing of the rod today, we wouldn't have so many spoiled children," he added.) Most of all, conservatives complained, courts had denied schools the most basic tool of moral order: religious instruction.[25]

Here right-wingers looked with special longing to one-room schools, noting—correctly—that most of them conducted prayers and Bible readings. As the 1975 Archie comic reminds us, earlier activists in the New Christian Right had already embraced the little red schoolhouse in their campaign against "Godless" public schools. But the movement received a boost from Reagan, who swept into the White House pledging to restore school prayer; at a famous campaign press conference, he also expressed doubts about the theory of evolution. In their paeans to the one-room school, then, conservatives increasingly cited its roots in religion— and the subsequent severing of this sacred bond. "In the America of an earlier day, Bible-reading and the 3 R's—ruin in Adam, redemption through Christ, and regeneration by the Holy Spirit—were not only permitted but expected," declared one right-wing minister in a 1986 issue of *Fundamentalist Journal*. The cover illustrated the moral costs of school secularization, showing disruptive children in a contemporary classroom. "Good Old Golden-Rule Days?" a headline asked, in a rhetorical nod to the one-room school. Although the little red schoolhouse taught children discipline and faith, another conservative wrote, both had been "sacrificed on the altar of political considerations." So in present-day public schools, a former teacher added, "all they learn is more deviltry."[26]

Not surprisingly, Americans of this bent increasingly exempted themselves from public education altogether. A boom began in Christian academies, which made up 11 percent of all private schools by 1989; four years later, the percentage had climbed to 15. Like other parochial schools, Christian academies tended to be small; in a handful of cases, indeed, they began with just a single room. The academies helped spark a modest revival of one-room schools in the 1980s and 1990s. Public single-teacher schools continued their steady decline, plummeting from 1,200 in 1984 to 429 a decade later. But the overall number of one-room schools held steady, balanced by the rise of private ones. The largest sector of growth lay in Amish schools, which flourished after the Supreme Court (in *Wisconsin v. Yoder,* 1972) exempted Amish children from compulsory education past eighth grade. The Amish accounted for more than 80 percent of private single-teacher schools by 1987, triggering yet another round of romanticized mass-media attention. "While the public one-room schools were becoming educational has-beens, the Plain People kept the old-fashioned little red school houses," one journalist wrote. Children prayed and studied "the unsweetened 3 Rs" from a special Amish textbook with a resonant title: the *Modern McGuffey Reader.* Another article illustrated the growth of these schools with a cartoon of a bearded Amish farmer, whose traditional black hat took a new shape: a little red schoolhouse.[27]

The one-room-school image also appeared prominently in the homeschool movement, one of the true growth industries in recent educational history. From only fifteen thousand in the early 1970s, the number of children taught at home rose to three hundred thousand in 1988 and had topped a million by the mid-1990s. Some homeschoolers used the little red schoolhouse as a negative referent, symbolizing the decline and degradation of public education writ large. "The little red schoolhouse has really become the little white sepulcher, and it's a seething cauldron of spiritual moral, and academic pathologies," declared one parent, in a 2004 attack on "humanistic and secular" public schools. Rather than indicting the one-room school, however, most homeschoolers invoked it. A Christian video company reached out to them with a Web site called "The Little Red Schoolhouse," complete with a red, slanted-roofed icon. Most remarkable, a "home makeover" reality television show erected a red building adjacent to a homeschooling family's new house. Furnished with familiar rows of desks and an American flag, the school bore an equally predictable name: The Little Red Schoolhouse.[28]

As the conservative 1980s gave way to the more moderate politics of the Bill Clinton era, American liberals also discovered a new affinity for the one-room school. Gone were the messianic tributes to open classrooms, which were widely regarded as a failure: by the early 1990s, one architect confirmed, most urban schools had returned to more traditional designs. But traces of the one-room school survived in new "cluster" plans, which grouped separate classrooms around a shared space, and, most of all, in new experiments with mixed-age instruction. Such efforts were "reminiscent of the romanticized little red schoolhouse of days gone by," one educator wrote in 1995; like the one-room school, they were "developmentally appropriate, untracked models of holistic, interdisciplinary, learner-centered classrooms." Some schools adopted nongraded classrooms by choice, invoking progressive-education gurus like John Dewey alongside popular accounts by Laura Ingalls Wilder, Louisa May Alcott, and others. But poorer districts—like the old one-room schools themselves—mixed grades out of economic necessity, not pedagogical philosophy. One New York school designed for seven hundred children enrolled twice that number, combining them into double or even triple classes; resistant at first, many teachers came to embrace the mixed-age model. "It's the little red school-house," said one fourth-grade instructor, who shared the school gym with two second-grade classes. "They've learned to concentrate better, and I think they're more sensitive to each other's needs."[29]

Most of all, the renewed liberal cult of the little red school-house buttressed a fresh educational consensus on the value of smaller schools. The trend was already apparent in the late 1970s and early 1980s, when citizens began to protest the growing size of public schools; citing E. F. Schumacher's classic countercultural text *Small Is Beautiful* (1973), several parent groups even formed their own one-room schools and demanded public funds. But it was private money—specifically, support from the computer titan Bill Gates—that catapulted the small-schools movement into a truly national force. In 2000, Gates pledged $15.7 million to help create ten small schools with no more than a hundred students per grade in Oakland, California. "The idea," wrote a local journalist, "is to bring back the little red school-house." By 2004, Gates's foundation had awarded $630 million to "downsize" schools around the country. More help came from the Clinton administration, which allocated $42 million in 2000 to establish Smaller Learning Communities in 354 districts. Spurred by charter-school legislation, which let private groups operate schools with public dollars, several towns in the rural West actually revived their one-room schools. News reports on these schools inevitably connected them to the small-school projects in urban districts, which were many times larger. As one reporter enthused, America's four hundred public one-room schools were "at once a nostalgic remnant of the past and a modern outlet for educational experimentation."[30]

Organizing Memory: The Dilemmas of Schoolhouse Preservation

More commonly, communities restored their old one-room schools for tourists. Another spate of schoolhouse preservation and living history programs arose in the 1990s, sponsored by a wide array of professional and citizen groups. Eleven universities restored one-room schools on their campuses, engaging alumni and other local boosters. Eastern Washington University received an abandoned schoolhouse from a nearby donor in exchange for four tickets to its football game against rival University of Montana. It also garnered $62,000 from a regional teachers union to mount the school on wheels and drive it to campus, which took two days and nights and generated extensive media coverage for the "schoolhouse on the move." At Central Michigan University, meanwhile, professor Alan Quick used a restored one-room school to conduct his graduate-level course in the history of education. Quick rang the school bell at 7:20 A.M., when students would take their seats in rows of small desks; he rang it again at 7:30 when they recited the Pledge of Allegiance. Then a student would play "School Days" on the piano, while everyone else sang along: "Readin' and 'ritin' and 'rith-

metic / Taught to the tune of a hickory stick." It made no difference that the song was written by an urban vaudevillian and
rarely sung in rural one-room schools; to Quick it captured the
"esprit de corps" that made the one-room school such a "great
learning environment."[31]

To others it was the hickory stick—that is, strict discipline—
that made the one-room school great. Indeed, restored schools
reflected the continued tension between conservative and liberal
visions of the little red schoolhouse. In 1983, at the height of the
Back to Basics movement, Northern Illinois University received
twelve hundred old schoolbooks and other educational memorabilia from former teacher Ruth Blackwell. To Blackwell, who attended and instructed one-room schools in South Dakota, her
artifacts symbolized the "old-fashioned" values, especially hard
work and discipline, that modern America had lost. "It is a shame
that we have taken away all rote teaching and memorization in
literature," Blackwell told an interviewer. "It is a teacher's duty
to give children what they need, not what they want." The university eventually moved Blackwell's collection to a restored
one-room schoolhouse on campus, where living-history programs moderated her conservative perspective with a more balanced one. By the late 1990s, when Illinois history standards had
recommended "a trip to a one-room schoolhouse," student visitors to the new Blackwell History of Education Museum learned
not only about harsh discipline but also about the progressive aspects of the one-room school. "Some of the techniques used in

the schoolhouse, such as peer tutoring, are still used in schools today," a museum leaflet explained.[32]

By the end of the 1990s, more than 450 restored one-room schools were open to the public in the United States; at least 25 of them bore the name Little Red Schoolhouse. Some of the projects were sponsored by local historical societies, which hired architects to restore the schools' original features; others were organized by informal citizens groups, who annoyed preservationists by repainting formerly white or gray schools red. "We're not polished professional people," explained one Oregon resident, who helped purchase and repair her local school. "Painting it to be historically perfect was not the most important criteria for a color choice." Not surprisingly, many of these citizens had attended one-room schools as children. In New York State, where more than 80 one-room-school projects were under way by 2004, roughly half the volunteers had a personal or familial connection to the school they restored; one-quarter had actually attended it themselves. Unlike the professional educators, who emphasized continuity between the little red schoolhouse and modern education, the elderly veterans of the one-room schools tended to focus on how much had been lost. "Our young people today don't have a clue of what we went through to get them to where they are today," worried a black volunteer in Maryland, working to restore a segregated one-room school. "And these are African-American kids. I see them clowning more than they are taking their work seriously."[33]

When students slacked off in the past, another black volunteer added, a slap of the ruler brought them back to task. More than any other theme, discipline dominated restoration and living-history efforts in the 1980s and 1990s. In part, one educator noted, this emphasis reflected a natural human interest: whatever their present-day viewpoints, visitors wanted to know how children were punished in the past. But it also reflected the background and ideology of restoration volunteers, who stressed the allegedly firm discipline of their own youth. "We had a lot of fun," wrote a sixth-grader in Avon, Connecticut, after a visit to a restored one-room school. "When we were bad we pretended to get switched by the teacher and wore the dunce hat." Another student noted that "discipline was a lot different"—and a lot better—in the old days. "Teachers don't really care about behavior today," she wrote, "and kids get away with a lot more." Ironically, the students' teacher hoped her pupils would appreciate the "coziness" and communal learning of the one-room schoolhouse. But their testimonials spoke only of corporal punishment, raising fears that living-history schoolmarms were practicing what they preached. "While historically accurate, corporal punishment SHOULD NOT be used in this program," warned one educator. "The interpreter may allude to, discuss, intimate, or threaten it . . . but to actually practice it is to place oneself in grave danger of prosecution for child abuse."[34]

Even as restored schools celebrated conservative values like discipline and order, meanwhile, these projects came into conflict with another basic American principle: the bottom line. Simply put, many citizens did not wish to invest in restoring old schools; they also resented the condescension of preservationists, who frequently came from outside the community. "It's often the old people who want to tear down their own history," surmised one observer from Ashfield, Massachusetts, "and the new people who want to preserve it." To newcomers, steeped in the culture of antiques collecting, Ashfield's old schoolhouse "just radiated identity—it said naively, proudly, *school*." But old-timers saw it as a decrepit reminder of past difficulties, and an expensive albatross to boot; stressing practicality over sentimentality, they voted to demolish it. A similar fate struck the old school in Winsted, Connecticut, where citizens turned down an impassioned appeal from the crusading lawyer—and school alumnus—Ralph Nader. "The public has spoken," Winsted's annoyed mayor declared. "People are getting quite fed up with the Naders telling us how to live." To Nader the demolition of the school was "like the loss of an old friend, a part of one's community roots." But the community itself wanted a modern school building, not an expensively renovated older one.[35]

Where citizens had purchased old schools for their own use, preservationists clashed with another deep-rooted American value: private property. Although many old schoolhouses were abandoned, others were put to creative—and commercial—purposes. Doctors reopened an Indiana one-room school as Old Schoolhouse Pediatrics; Michigan patrons rang the bell of the

Schoolhouse Ice Cream Parlor until neighbors complained of the noise; Pennsylvanians ate at the Little Red Schoolhouse diner, complete with specials written on the original blackboard; and in South Huntington, New York, officials sold their historic one-room school to the Bagel Nosh restaurant chain. "The fare at the 'little red schoolhouse' here used to be reading, 'riting and 'rithmetic on hardwood desks with inkwells," a local journalist wrote. "Soon it will be nova or lox on bagels with cream cheese." ("You hate to see a landmark go, but I do understand the economics and the practicality of the sale," the school's principal added. "Besides, I like bagels.") Such developments sent shudders up the spines of professional preservationists, who valued the schools' original design. But private owners rejected this position as "sterile and static," to quote one observer, and preferred preserving their schools through adaptive re-use. By converting an old school to new purposes, they argued, Americans could respect the past even as they prepared for the future.[36]

Most of all, Americans transformed one-room schools into family homes. "Nostalgia is 'in' for folks who remember, restore, and relish the one-room charm," wrote one observer in 1993, noting the growing trend in school-to-home conversions. "For many, one-room schools are a tangible connection to a way of life and education that seems simpler (and perhaps better in this age of funding crisis and reform controversy)." One Michigan school owner claimed she could still smell chili and baking bread in a corner of her house where students had heated their lunches on a potbellied stove; another said he heard the ghost of a former teacher who had reportedly committed suicide in the school. In isolated cases, meanwhile, older Americans came to live in the same schools they had attended as children. In Pennsylvania, one retiree restored the red brick school where he went to first and second grade; fifty years later, a local reporter wrote, he was "learning a different three R's: renovating, remodeling, and redecorating." He planned to divide the 26-by-28-foot space into five rooms and remove the blackboards, which would be donated to a "real" one-room schoolhouse: the nearby Amish school, where children of different ages still studied under a single teacher.[37]

Not surprisingly, then, few schoolhouses met the stringent standards of authenticity that preservationists sought. In 1994 just 6 percent of the sites on the National Register of Historic Places—which required buildings to retain certain original features—concerned education, and only a fraction of these buildings were one-room schools. Six years later, the National Trust for Historic Preservation named "Historic Neighborhood Schools" one of its annual "11 Most Endangered Places." It included multi-story urban buildings as well as one-room schools, which fell victim to "policies promoting the construction of mega-schools." Corning, New York, closed three small schools in favor of a new consolidated building five miles outside town, near a proposed Wal-Mart; in Santa Fe, four older schools faced demolition after officials deemed them "amenity challenged." Schools that closed went quickly to seed, especially in rural areas. Of the two hundred thousand one-room schools that operated in 1900, twelve thousand still stood by the mid-1990s. Most of them were abandoned and rotting, victimized by arsonists as well as natural forces. "Like a forgotten friend it remains here alone, / Filled only with sounds of the wind as it moans," wrote one Michigan woman about her old school. "It seems such a shame that this country shrine / Has stood here neglected for such a long time."[38]

So citizens took it upon themselves to preserve the memory of the one-room school, even as its physical frame changed into barns, stores, and homes or disappeared altogether. Founded in 1993, the Michigan One-Room Schoolhouse Association and the Society for the Preservation of Ohio One-Room Schools conducted surveys of one-room schools and provided information about restorations, museums, and living history projects. At the national level, the Country School Association sponsored an annual conference and an online newsletter for curators, authors, photographers, and former teachers. Meanwhile, so-called nostalgia magazines—especially *Good Old Days*, *Reminisce*, and *Capper's*—solicited readers' recollections of the one-room school, keeping the little red schoolhouse alive in other ways. Magazines published special issues on the subject and often reprinted them as books, which in turn generated more "memory letters" from their largely white, senior-citizen audience. In 1993, for example, *Capper's* released *My Folks and the One-Room Schoolhouse*, the latest in its successful *My Folks* series; previous volumes bore titles like

My Folks Came in a Covered Wagon and *My Folks Claimed the Plains.*
As an editor recounted, introducing the schoolhouse book, the
call by *Capper's* for "true tales of readers' experiences" had "garnered a wonderful response." Yet these reminiscences hardly
told the whole story, she happily admitted, or even half of it. "By
collecting these warm and often funny stories, we intend to preserve the heritage of the one-room schoolhouses," she wrote.
"We make no claim of complete historical accuracy; these are
purely personal glimpses into the past as it is remembered by
those who lived it."[39]

Finally, still other Americans used their cameras to safeguard
the memory of the one-room school. In Otsego County, New
York, housepainter John Hall resolved to record pictures of all
333 one-room schoolhouses that had operated in the county
a century earlier. Known around the area as "School House
John," Hall took Polaroid photographs of every standing schoolhouse he could locate; for the buildings that had disappeared he
searched out old postcards or pictures. Hall studied maps and
books to identify schools, but his best sources were the county's
senior citizens. "There isn't much sense in my talking to anyone under 30," Hall noted. "You've got to be at least 65, really,
to have had anything to do with one-room schools." Hall also
engaged in some "friendly competition" with neighboring
Delaware County, where a similar quest was under way. Other
hobbyists made their way across the country, shooting photographs of any one-room school they encountered. By 1998, Ari-

zona retiree Mary Kimmel and her husband, William, had taken pictures of eight hundred schools—abandoned, readapted, and restored—in twenty-one states. "When we photograph a refurbished schoolhouse museum, I can almost hear the bells from my childhood ringing again," noted Mary Kimmel, who had attended a one-room school. She also collected replicas of one-room schools, including red slanted-roofed music boxes that played "School Days."[40]

The rise of the Internet helped fuel a brisk trade in these figurines along with original schoolhouse furniture, providing yet another medium for Americans to remember their one-room schools. The biggest purchasers were probably owners of converted schools, who decorated their homes with slate backboards, school desks, and other vintage items. Americans also collected objects from their own one-room schools or from their parents' and grandparents' schools, establishing a deeply personal link to the past. "I just found one of my Momma's boxes with slate pencils inside," one Oklahoma reader wrote to *Capper's*. "What a thrill!" Another reader gazed admiringly at the handbell used by his father, a one-room-school teacher in Kentucky. "Strange, isn't it, how a simple object like a schoolbell seems, at times, to be a living thing," he wrote. "I'm sure some of the children who were in my father's care can still hear the bell's merry ting-a-ling whenever they recall their happy school days." A former Indiana teacher proudly displayed her own handbell, which a great-aunt had used a century before. At a 1992 one-room-school reunion a former Michigan teacher used her original bell to call alumni to dinner. It mattered little that the teacher had actually purchased the bell in Cape Cod in the 1950s after her school installed an electric buzzer. Like the school-shaped music box that played "School Days," a song that few rural students ever sang, the bell reverberated in America's collective imagination. It rang out, loud and clear, for the one-room school that Americans wanted to remember.[41]

Dear Old Golden Rule Days?

In 2000, the Arizona historian Michael F. Anderson wrote a foreword for the first comprehensive guide to America's restored one-room schoolhouses. A respected scholar of the West and the National Park System, Anderson began with the best-known lines about the American one-room school: "School days, school days/Dear old golden rule days/Reading and 'Riting and 'Rithmetic..." Then he paused. "I don't know who penned the verse, nor do I remember the rest," Anderson wrote, "but I can imagine the songwriter with wrinkled brow and wistful smile lost in memories, perhaps casting his or her mind's eye back to a rural setting, a one-room, log or frame building with a bell clanging and children romping in the schoolyard." Alas, Anderson's own recollections resembled nothing in the song. "Myself, I look back to a multi-room, suburban school with irritating buzzers," he admitted. But that was all the more reason to preserve one-room schools and the memories that attached to them, even if these memories were not always historically accurate. "This book might have been titled 'Little Red,' because when we think of America's one-room schoolhouses, our minds tell us these are— or should be—little red schoolhouses." Most one-room schools were painted white or yellow or brown, Anderson acknowledged, if they were painted at all.[1]

Like the three hundred so-called "schoolhouse museums" in the guide, Anderson's clever foreword reminds us how history and memory work together to color—literally and figuratively— the one-room school. "School Days" was composed by a German immigrant, Gus Edwards, who spent most of his life in New York City and probably never set foot in a country school. Whereas Anderson imagined him "lost in memories" of a rural childhood, then, Edwards was himself imagining the one-room schoolhouse based on *other* contemporary memories—the poems, pictures, and tales that Edwards had seen and heard. Yet after his song became popular, it structured the way future generations visualized the school days of old. Although Anderson attended a bland suburban school with annoying buzzers, he could easily envision the clanging bell and the romping schoolchildren of the one-room rural school. So can most Americans, no matter where they were educated.

They also imagine the school painted red, even though, as Anderson noted, it usually wasn't. Illuminating the process of collective memory, his comments also point to the inevitable distortions it can produce. The most obvious mistakes concern the physical appearance of the one-room school, which was seldom tidy, quaint, or comfortable. The buildings varied widely in quality as well as color: Massachusetts and New York spent more than a hundred dollars per child each year on school improvements in the 1913, while Mississippi spent just four. But few schools matched the idyllic image of the Little Red Schoolhouse, where the stove was always hot, the windows were always clean, and the roof was always in good repair. Nor can this icon capture the huge range of building materials and designs that characterized America's two hundred thousand one-room schools. Nebraska pioneers built a 16-by-12-foot school from straw, which cattle ate two years later; a Kansas teacher held her first school in a sod dugout, using a stick to etch lessons on the dirt floor; and in California, the poet Edwin Markham taught a so-called "brush school" at an oak tree encircled by branches. At the other end of the spectrum, wealthier schools added Gothic-style arched windows or Greek Revival pillars. Yet the little red schoolhouse collapsed these differences into a single ideal type, which rarely, if ever, corresponded to reality.[2]

Nor did Americans' frequent paeans to the school's instruction, which distorted the past in other ways. Despite the shared visual image of the little red schoolhouse, Americans remembered different aspects of the education they received there. By necessity, then, they forgot others; as the French philosopher Ernest Renan observed over a century ago, the two activities always proceed in tandem. Especially in the United States—and still more, at the academy—Americans tend to think of this dynamic as a conservative or even reactionary one: the right wants to preserve a sunny and simple past, while the left seeks to restore its historical complexities. As this book has shown, however, the tendency is endemic to both. Whatever their political or pedagogical bent, Americans have imagined a little red schoolhouse to suit it. Unavoidably, then, they have exaggerated certain dimensions of the one-room school and downplayed others. That does not make them manipulative, or cynical, or evil. It simply makes them human. We all tailor the past to serve the present, all the time. But Americans are probably more likely to do it when they encounter an icon like the little red schoolhouse, which is so widely shared and loved. Just as they have altered the memory of George Washington or Abraham Lincoln in light of latter-day events, so have they distorted the one-room school.[3]

For liberals, I have shown, these distortions most often surround the ideal of cooperative teaching and learning. From Dorothy Canfield Fisher in the Progressive era to open-classroom activists in the 1960s, left-leaning Americans have celebrated the little red schoolhouse as the locus of communalism in education: where the big city school divides and alienates, the argument goes, the small rural school unites and nurtures. At its most extreme, this vision even supposes that the one-room school pioneered the inclusion of mentally handicapped children. "'Mainstreaming' is an education-world buzz-word today," wrote one liberal enthusiast in 1978, "but rural teachers have always worked with the whole range of student abilities, from the very slow to the very quick, without putting labels on the process." History says otherwise. One-room schools ranked children constantly, through spelling bees and other competitions; they often labeled children "dull," "slow," or even "retarded"; and the most mentally challenged children were not allowed to attend school at all. In the early 1950s, one Iowa community established a special class for "trainable retarded children" in an abandoned one-room schoolhouse. But even this exceptional case segregated the children instead of mainstreaming them, liberal fantasies notwithstanding. As a liberal myself, I too wish that the one-room school had been truly inclusive of the handicapped. But as a historian, I know that it was not.[4]

More generally, I also know that children did not teach one another with as much freedom—or as much success—as some one-room-school devotees suppose. Facing so many students of different ages and abilities, most teachers tried to enforce silence over everything else; indeed, one nineteenth-century teacher wrote, a quiet classroom was considered "the very summit of pedagogical excellence." When children assisted one another, then, they were probably more often punished than praised. Consider the 1986 poem by Jane Kenyon, "Trouble with Math in a One-Room Country School," which recalls Kenyon's rural Michigan education. Confused by a long-division problem, she asks for help from a student who sits next to her. The teacher is not pleased, to say the least:

> Miss Moran sprang from her monumental desk
> And led me roughly through the class
> without a word. My shame was radical
> as she propelled me past the cloakroom
> to the furnace closet, where only the boys
> were put, only the older ones at that.
> The door swung briskly shut
>
> The warmth, the gloom, the smell
> of sweeping compound clinging to the broom
> soothed me. I found a bucket, turned it
> upside down, and sat, hugging my knees.
> I hummed a theme from Haydn that I knew
> from my piano lessons . . .
> and hardened my heart against authority.
> And then I heard her steps, her fingers
> on the latch. She led me, blinking
> and changed, back to the class. [Ellipsis in original.][5]

Recounted bitterly by the liberal Kenyon, episodes like this are recalled with pride by many conservatives. To right-leaning

Americans, in fact, strict discipline represents one of the chief virtues of the one-room school. Yet when conservatives imagine a schoolhouse of quiet obedience, they distort the past every bit as much as liberals who celebrate freedom and cooperative learning. To be sure, many teachers tried to govern by an iron fist—or, as we have seen, a wooden switch. As often as not, however, they failed: our histories are replete with descriptions of rowdy classrooms, where the "big boys" ruled the roost. Nor did parents always support the teacher, as many Americans still like to believe. "Teachers stood for A and D—Authority and Discipline, with capital letters," recalled Mabel Anthony, a retiree from Michigan. "Teachers and parents were solidly aligned and prevarication only postponed punishment." Perhaps her own school was exceptional; or, like most of us, she described the school that she wanted to remember. Hardly a paradigm of order, the one-room school was a cauldron of chaos and, most of all, of contestation: teachers faced off against students in a never-ending war for control. "Such life-and-death struggles are as inseparably associated with the little red schoolhouse as they are with the ruins of the Roman amphitheater," wrote one educator in 1894. "As the early Christians were stretched over slow fires, and stung to death by bees, and torn to pieces by wild beasts, so the young man beginning a term in a new school expected to be tormented by the older boys."[6]

Since then, Americans have celebrated the rural "bad boy" in story and song: think of Tom Sawyer removing his teacher's wig with a cat, or Henry Ford urging students to fire soybeans at instructors with a peashooter. In the same breath as they extol the firm discipline of the one-room school, indeed, contemporary conservatives look back fondly on its pranks and mischief. Exalting the "Authority and Discipline" of her old school, for example, Mabel Anthony also delighted in the tomfoolery of her classmates. "While one grade recited, seven others studied previously assigned chapters—when they weren't passing notes, throwing spitballs or poking toes through the seat ahead," Anthony recalled. Another Michigan woman recounted her father's stories about a particularly strict schoolmarm, the evocatively named "Sadie" Reuschlein, who whipped miscreants with a rubber hose. The boys would fill it with chalk, which flew all over the school when Reuschlein took her first swing. "It may have been funny to the kids in the classroom," the woman wrote, "but it probably didn't lessen the number of blows that the unruly kid was about to receive." The chalk-filled hose provides a vivid metaphor for the paradoxical way many Americans envision the one-room school: it was authoritarian and mischievous, all at the same time.[7]

How could it be both? At the level of logic—even more, of history—it would seem impossible: the classroom could not be perfectly regimented and also full of high jinks. But at the level of memory, it makes perfect sense. The strict teacher needs the unruly student, and vice versa, for each to play his or her assigned role in America's imagined educational drama. To act as the stern taskmaster Sadie Reuschlein required disobedient children; to give her rubber hose a target the children had to disobey. And

while current-day student misbehavior is seen as deeply threatening—think of juvenile delinquents, gangbangers, and school
shooters—the old-style pranks are all remembered as good fun.
This is why the audience laughed at *Sugar Babies*, the 1979 Broadway hit featuring lines from an old burlesque sketch called "The
Little Red Schoolhouse": the naughty boy ribbed the schoolmarm, she rolled up a newspaper to swat him, and everyone went
home happy. "We were told 'Spare the rod and spoil the child,'
and our teachers and parents lived by it," wrote one contributor
to *Good Old Days*, a popular nostalgia magazine. "It has left us
with many memories, more humorous than terrible." An accompanying Norman Rockwell–style illustration shows a student
writing "I was a bad boy" on the blackboard, over and over again.
But he is grinning, all the while, and so do readers. "Priceless
Memories of Those Dear Old Golden Rule Days," advertised a
compilation by *Reminisce*, another nostalgia magazine, "from folks
who 'learned to the tune of a hickory stick' and smile when they
recall it."[8]

The advertising come-on brings us back to the question of
nostalgia itself, a modern disease that afflicts us all. If the past is a
foreign country, as the historian David Lowenthal has written,
nostalgia has given it a boundless tourist trade: we all yearn for
something in the past, whether we admit it or not. Nobody wants
to be known as nostalgic, of course, which connotes a childish
longing for lost innocence. Grow up, we tell ourselves; get over
it; get real. But we can never quite do so, returning again and

again to the primal scenes of our youth: home, family, and—yes—school. Like Michael Anderson, and Gus Edwards before him, most Americans "remember" one-room-school days only through the memory of others. Whether they actually attended the institution or not, however, all are influenced by the romantic spirit that envelops it. "Perhaps I'm drunk on nostalgia," wrote the *New York Times* columnist Nicholas Kristof in 2003, after a visit to a one-room school in South Dakota, "but I believe we should push harder to create small schools." Having attended a small multigrade school himself, Kristof selected his metaphor well: like alcohol, nostalgia inevitably skews our perceptions. It makes the past look so good that we want to return there, leaving the present behind. "If I could hear that bell toll / once more before I died," wrote one woman, in a 1993 ode to the one-room school, "I'd think I was in heaven / with St. Peter in the sky." Another former student was less lyrical, but equally sentimental. "At the ringing of a school bell," he flatly declared, "I would start first grade tomorrow."[9]

But he cannot, of course, and neither can we. The drunken high of nostalgia is inevitably followed by a sober morning hangover, when we realize that we will never be home again. Nor is it always clear that we would return, even if we could: you can miss a place desperately without really wanting to go back there. Consider the 1996 poem by Joyce Carol Oates, who went to a one-room school in upstate New York:

Crumbling stone steps of the old schoolhouse
Boarded-up windows shards of winking glass
Built 1898, numerals faint in stone as shadow
Through a window, obedient rows of desks mute
Only a droning of hornets beneath the eaves,
The cries of red-winged blackbirds by the creek

How many generations of this rocky countryside grown &
    gone
How many memories & all forgotten
No one to chronicle, no regret

& the schoolhouse soon to be razed & goodbye to America
The flagless pole, what a relief!
I love it, the eye lifting skyward to nothing
Never to pledge allegiance to the United States of America
    again
Never to press my flat right hand over my heart again as if I
    had one.

Oates's verse continues a long tradition of bittersweet schoolhouse
poetry, going back to John Greenleaf Whittier. The author returns to the fulcrum of youth, only to discover that it is decaying;
soon it will be gone, along with all of the memories that permeate
it. Like Jane Kenyon, who recounted her punishment in a closet,
Oates is under no illusions about the one-room school itself. "Can
one be nostalgic for a world in which, in fact, one would not wish

to live, as for incidents one would not wish to relive?" Oates asked several years later, noting the "stab of emotion" she received when recalling her old school. The question answered itself. "I would not wish any child I know to endure such experiences," she concluded, "yet I could not imagine my own life without them." Hence the title of her schoolhouse poem: "Nostalgia."[10]

For the historian, meanwhile, nostalgia poses another problem. When it distorts the past, should we attempt to set the record straight? If nostalgia is really "memory with the pain removed," to quote David Lowenthal again, should we try to put the pain back in? That was the dilemma of the Nebraska scholar Sandy Scofield, one of the Country School Legacy researchers who discovered that her seminar audience wished only to hear about the virtues of rural schools. "Nostalgia has a legitimate place and that seems to be what appeals to these groups so I'm not sure how much I should push for fear of alienating them," confided Scofield. "I'm tempted to say—'they're enjoying themselves—why fight it?'" For the elderly, especially, warm images of the one-room school connected them to their old communities, families, and selves. "I've always been a firm believer in not dwelling on the past," wrote one New Yorker, in a standard apologia for schoolhouse nostalgia, "but sometimes it gives you a serendipitous lift to slip back to those rose-hued memories of childhood and linger for just a little while." Why fight it?[11]

One answer goes back to the Progressives, who argued that romantic portrayals of one-room schools would interfere with school consolidation and other needed educational improvements. The battle was fought anew in 1980 in Nebraska, where about three hundred of the nation's nine-hundred-odd one-room schools continued to operate. "There are unfortunately a number, an appalling number, of one-room country schools *still* in existence in Nebraska, with outdoor privies, incredibly slipshod teaching, with a criminal lack of books and other teaching tools," wrote state school board member and historian Dorothy Weyer Creigh in support of a bill to close the schools. "I know the present-day one-room country schools for the anachronisms they are, and I am eager to dispel the myth of the rural schools now as the be-all and end-all of educational excellence." Myth or not, Nebraskans believed it. The bill died in committee, and its author lost his bid for reelection; five years later, when a new consolidation bill made it through the legislature, voters overturned it in a referendum. Not until 2005 did the state finally pass a law to consolidate rural districts, this time over the veto of the governor. According to press reports, legislators closed the small districts mainly because they had become tax shelters for landowners who did not want to pay for high schools. But Nebraskans continued to venerate the one-room school itself, which was an icon that no politician risked attacking.[12]

More recently, educators have worried that sentimentalizing the little red schoolhouse lays the groundwork for vouchers and other privatization schemes. "The romantic notion of a trouble-free past is as old as the legend of the Garden of Eden before the

Fall," wrote the veteran scholar and reformer Michael P. Riccards in 2004. Worshiping the "halcyon days of the past" was a "flight into nostalgia" that could only end in a major crash for public education itself: by downplaying or ignoring every problem or difficulty of yesteryear, schoolhouse nostalgia made current public schools seem beyond repair. To be sure, privatization advocates have recently invoked the little red schoolhouse; at least one pro-voucher organization, Putting Children First, uses it as an official logo. As we have seen, however, every educational partisan in America has tried to seize this image. No side has captured it; even more, the sides keep changing. When Ronald Reagan ran for president, critics mocked his proposal to eliminate the Department of Education as "nostalgia for the little red schoolhouse"; yet four years later, when Reagan's threat had proved empty, a principals' association presented him with a birthday cake shaped like a little red schoolhouse. And as we saw in the first lines of this book, Reagan's own Republican Party decorated the entrances to the Department of Education with, yes, little red schoolhouses. Nostalgia for the one-room school surely distorts history, in more ways than I have recounted here. But it also connects Americans to a shared past, even as they embellish—or ignore—various aspects of it.[13]

Indeed, despite Americans' many differences, the little red schoolhouse might be the only icon that can bring them together. Regardless of the lumps it has taken of late, public education remains the major venue in which to discuss and deliberate the values Americans wish to transmit to their children. So if they want to make it more democratic—or more effective, or more rigorous, or more inclusive, or more *anything*—they will need a collective ideal. The little red schoolhouse provides it. Consider the cartoon by Ben Sargent in the wake of the Columbine school shooting of 1999, when two Colorado boys gunned down thirteen people and then took their own lives. Sargent drew a one-room school under fire, and for the caption he offered his own version of "School Days":

> School days, school days,
> Packin' heat is cool days
> We'd read and we'd write
> and we'd hit the ground
> At the tell tale whine
> of a magnum round
> You packed a Raven .25
> A 9-millimeter was more my style
> Who'd ever have thought
> we would both survive
> Being a couple of kids?

Every American could look at this cartoon and know immediately what Sargent meant. So did readers who saw a 2006 cartoon of a little red schoolhouse under "lunatic alert," after a Pennsylvania man killed five Amish girls at a genuine single-teacher school.[14] They all recognized the shape of the one-room school and its classic bell tower, which helped underscore the tragedy of these events in ways that no other emblem could. However much it distorts the past, the little red schoolhouse ideal reflects the best in American education. Anyone who wants to build a better future will have to start there.

Notes

Introduction

1. "Paige Fields Team to Leave No Child Left Behind," U.S. Department of Education Press Release, 11 April 2002, at http://www.ed.gov/news/pressreleases/2002/04/04112002a.html; Erik W. Robelen, "Federal File," *Education Week*, 17 April 2002, 25.

2. Andrew Shain, "2 Days to Go," *Charlotte Observer*, 5 November 2006; Christopher Knight for School Board Advertisement # 1, http://www.youtube.com/watch?v=nLi5BoIefsk, accessed 7 April 2008.

3. http://cgi.ebay.com/Sterling-LITTLE-RED-SCHOOL-HOUSE-Enamel-Charm_W0QQitemZ260101524987QQcmdZViewItem, accessed 21 August 2007; "A slender lifeline," *Philadelphia Inquirer*, 18 July 2007.

4. See John Bodnar, *Remaking America: Public Memory, Commemoration, and Patriotism in the Twentieth Century* (Princeton, N.J.: Princeton University Press, 1992), esp. 13–14.

5. "Filling a Child's Needs as the School Bell Rings," *New York Times*, 1 September 1984; "Little Red Schoolhouse," http://lrshlansing.com, accessed 21 August 2007; Gwenyth Swain, "Revisiting the One-Room School," *Book Links*, March 2005, 14–17.

6. Robert Nisbet, *History of the Idea of Progress* (1980; New Brunswick, N.J.: Transaction, 1994), 4–5; Fred Davis, *Yearning for Yesterday: A Sociology of Nostalgia* (New York: Free Press, 1979), 116; David Lowenthal, *The Past Is a Foreign Country* (Cambridge: Cambridge University Press, 1985), 10–11; Svetlana Boym, *The Future of Nostalgia* (New York: Basic, 2001), xiii.

7. "Small School, Big Challenges," *Minneapolis Star-Tribune*, 27 January 2002; Robbie Branscum, *To the Tune of a Hickory Stick* (Garden City, N.Y.: Doubleday, 1978), 68; Christopher B. Manaseri, "Keeping School: One-Room Schoolhouse Preservation Projects in the Greater Finger Lakes Region of New York State" (Ph.D. diss., Syracuse University, 2004), 254.

8. *One Room Country Schools: South Dakota Stories*, ed. Norma C. Wilson and Charles L. Woodard (Brookings: South Dakota Humanities Foundation, 1998), 132; Fern Small, "The Passing of Gliddenburg School" (ms, n.d. [1993]), "Gliddenburg-Grubtown" binder, Bess Britton Michigan One-Room Schoolhouse Collection, Van Buren District Library, Decatur, Michigan.

9. Dean Foster, "History of the Keeler School" (ms, n.d. [1993?]), 4–5, "K" binder, Britton Collection; "Note from Barbara Bush," in Andrew Gulliford, *America's Country Schools*, 3rd ed. (Boulder: University Press of Colorado, 1996), 5.

10. Alice F. Suroski to Andrew Gulliford, 23 December 1980, folder 31, box 10, Country School Legacy Collection, University Archives, University of Colorado Libraries, Boulder; William Pless, "Reminisces of a Childhood" (ms, n.d.), 5, "Gage-Glidden" binder, Britton Collection.

ONE

The One-Room Schoolhouse as History

1. Michael V. O'Shea, "The Passing of the District School," in *School Buildings and Grounds*, ed. William Kirk Fowler (Lincoln, Neb.: Department of Public Instruction, 1902), 234; O'Shea, *Education as Adjustment: Educational Theory Viewed in the Light of Contemporary Thought*, 3rd ed. (New York: Longman, Green, 1906), 145.

2. Quoted in William Gould Vinal, *The Rise and Fall of Ye District School in Plimouth Plantation (1800–1900)* (Norwell, Mass.: Vinehall, 1958), 57.

3. Andrew Gulliford, *America's Country Schools*, 3rd ed. (Boulder: Univer-

sity Press of Colorado, 1996), 35; Wayne E. Fuller, *One-Room Schools of the Middle West: An Illustrated History* (Lawrence: University Press of Kansas, 1994), 104; *One-Teacher Schools Today* (Washington, D.C.: Research Division, National Education Association, 1960), 9.

4. "Teacher Leaving, School Will Shut," *New York Times*, 2 April 1957; "New Canaan Pride Is One-Room School," *New York Times*, 10 September 1953.

5. Carl Kaestle, *Pillars of the Republic: Common Schools and American Society, 1780–1860* (New York: Hill and Wang, 1983), 13; David B. Tyack, *The One Best System: A History of American Urban Education* (Cambridge: Harvard University Press, 1974); Claudia Goldin and Lawrence F. Katz, "The 'Virtues' of the Past: Education in the First Hundred Years of the Republic," National Bureau of Economic Research, Working Paper 9958 (September 2003), 1–3.

6. Goldin and Katz, " 'Virtues' of the Past," 12; Sun Go and Peter H. Lindert, "The Curious Dawn of American Public Schools," National Bureau of Economic Research, Working Paper 13335 (August 2007), 7, 20.

7. Carl Wheeless, *Landmarks of American Presidents* (New York: Gale, 1996), 30, 155, 206; Sue Thomas, *A Second Home: Missouri's Early Schools* (Columbia: University of Missouri Press, 2006), 40; Myrna J. Grove, *Legacy of One-Room Schools* (Morgantown, Penn.: Masthof Press, 2000), 15; Leslie C. Swanson, *Rural One-Room Schools of Mid-America* (Moline, Ill.: Leslie Swanson, 1976), 36; Alan S. Brown, "The Northwest Ordinance and Michigan's Quest for Excellence in Education," *Michigan History* 71 (Nov.–Dec. 1987): 26–27.

8. "School Architecture," *American Journal of Education* 9 (December 1860): 505; James Johonnot, *School-Houses* (New York: J. W. Schermerhorn, 1871), 14; Warren A. Henke, "Preface," in *The Legacy of North Dakota's Country Schools*, ed. Warren A. Henke and Everett C. Albers (Bismarck: North Dakota Humanities Council, 1998), iv; Daniel Tysen Smith, "Appalachia's Last One-Room School: A Case Study" (Ph.D. diss., University of Kentucky, 1988), 14; "The Truth About 'The Little Red School,'" *World's Work* 26 (1913): 228; Howard M. Etter to Albert Mason, 14 August 1973, Little Red Schoolhouse Collection, University Archives, Lehman Library, Shippensburg University, Shippensburg, Pennsylvania.

9. "Seldom Heard of Now: The 'Little Red Schoolhouse' No More a Political Issue," *New York Times*, 22 October 1916; Vinal, *Rise and Fall of Ye*

District School, 28; Gerald J. Stout, *Requiem for the Little Red Schoolhouse* (Athol, Mass.: Athol Press, 1987), 39; Joanne Raetz Stuttgen, "(Re)constructing the Little Red Schoolhouse: History, Landscape, and Memory" (Ph.D. diss., Indiana University, 2002), 194; Letha Fuller, "The Compromise," in *The Little Country Schoolhouse* (Berne, Ind.: House of White Birches, 1996), 11; "Georgia State Federation of Women's Clubs," *Atlanta Constitution*, 17 December 1922; "Political Notes," *New York Times*, 13 November 1890.

10. William A. Alcott, *Essay on the Construction of School-Houses* (Boston: Hillard, Gray, Little and Wilkins, 1832), 13–14; "Schools as They Were in the United States, Sixty and Seventy Years Ago" *American Journal of Education* 16 (1866): 130; Johonnot, *School-Houses*, 23; *Country School Legacy: Humanities on the Frontier* (Silt, Colo.: Country School Legacy, 1981), 11; Severance Burrage and Henry Turner Bailey, *School Sanitation and Decoration: A Practical Study of Health and Beauty in Their Relations to the Public Schools* (Boston: Heath, 1899), 29–30; Fletcher B. Dresslar, *American Schoolhouses* (Washington, D.C.: Government Printing Office, 1911), 123; Fuller, *One-Room Schools of the Middle West*, 21–23; A. E. Gray, "First-Year Teacher," in *Good Old Days Remembers the Little Country Schoolhouse*, ed. Ken Tate and Janice Tate (Berne, Ind.: House of White Birches, 1999), 63.

11. Clifton Johnson, *Old-Time Schools and School Books* (1904; New York: Dover, 1963), 104; "Schools as They Were in the United States," 135, 130; Kaestle, *Pillars of the Republic*, 16; James D. MacConnell, *Dr. Mac, Planner for Schools* (Palo Alto, Calif.: Johnson/Dole, 1988), 9; Thomas D. Clark, *My Century in History* (Lexington: University of Kentucky Press, 2006), 26; "School Architecture," 519; Mary Hurlbut Cordier, "Prairie Schoolwomen, Mid-1850s to 1920s, in Iowa, Kansas, and Nebraska," *Great Plains Quarterly* 8 (Spring 1988): 109.

12. "School Architecture," 496, 497; A C. Washburn to Henry Barnard, "Monroe Notes on HB, 1840–41" folder, series 3, Henry Barnard Papers, Fales Library, New York University; *The United States School Room: Improved Arrangement of School Desks* (n.p., n.d. [1856]), pp. 2–3, "Schools and Correspondence Schools—Misc." folder; Baker, Pratt, and Company, School Furnishers, *Our New Folding-Lid Study Desk* (n.p., n.d. [1870]), pp. 2–4, "School Supplies A–G" folder, both in box 5, Romaine Trade Catalogue Collection, Special Collections, Davidson Library, University of California, Santa Barbara; James P. Logan, "An Old-Time

Pedagogue: Memories of a Country District School in Civil War Days," *Proceedings of the New Jersey Historical Society*, n.d. [1935], p. 265, folder 1, box 11, Country School Legacy Collection, University Archives, University of Colorado Libraries, Boulder.

13. "Education and Educational Institutions," *American Journal of Education* 32 (1882): 971; Fred A. Williams, *The Educational Red Book: A Buyer's Guide for School Superintendents, Secretaries and Members of Boards of Education* (Albany: C. F. Williams, 1922), 10–11; Faith Dunne, "Choosing Smallness: An Examination of the Small School Experience in Rural America," in *Education in Rural America: A Reassessment of the Conventional Wisdom*, ed. Jonathan P. Sher (Boulder, Colo.: Westview, 1977), 88; Wayne E. Fuller, *The Old Country School* (Chicago: University of Chicago Press, 1982), 76; Richard J. Ellis, *To the Flag: The Unlikely History of the Pledge of Allegiance* (Lawrence: University Press of Kansas, 2005), 2–3; Jesse Knowlton Flanders, *Legislative Control of the Elementary Curriculum* (New York: Teachers College Press, 1925), 52–53; School Improvement Association of South Carolina, *Bulletin II* (Columbia: State Company Printers, 1907), 28, "Rural Schools/ School Improvement" folder, box 24, Liberty Hyde Bailey Papers, Rare Book and Manuscript Collections, Cornell University, Ithaca, New York; Curt Davis, *Forty Years in the One-Room Schools of Eastern Kentucky: A Memoir*, ed. Laura Caudill (Ashland, Ky.: Jesse Stuart Foundation, 2001), 18.

14. "School-House Architecture—No. 2," *New England Journal of Education* 3 (18 March 1876): 134, quoted in Nicolai Cikovsky, Jr., "Winslow Homer's *School Time*: 'A Picture Thoroughly National,'" in *In Honor of Paul Mellon*, ed. John Wilmerding (Washington, D.C.: National Gallery of Art, 1986), 68n22; "School Architecture," 520, 493; Ruth Zinar, "Educational Problems in Rural Vermont, 1875–1900: A Not So Distant Mirror," *Vermont History* 51 (Fall 1983): 204; Clifton Johnson, *The Country School in New England* (New York: D. Appleton, 1893), 50; *My Folks and the One-Room Schoolhouse: A Treasury of One-Room School Stories Shared by Capper's Readers* (Topeka, Kan.: Capper Press, 1993), 57.

15. "School Architecture," 505, 502; Fuller, *Old Country School*, 73; Paul Theobald, *Call School: Rural Education in the Midwest to 1918* (Carbondale: Southern Illinois University Press, 1995), 133; Thomas, *Second Home*, 48–49; Edna M. Hill, "The Little Red Schoolhouse a 'Fake,'" *Independent* (7 August 1913): 317; John R. Kirk, "The Best Rural School Building in America" (ms, 1911), 3, John R. Kirk Papers, Special Collec-

tions, Pickler Memorial Library, Truman State University, Kirksville, Missouri.

16. Thomas, *Second Home*, 58–59; William A. Degregorio, *The Complete Book of United States Presidents*, 3rd ed. (New York: Wings, 1991), 107; Enos J. Perry, *The Boyhood Days of Our Presidents* (n.p.: Enos J. Perry, 1971), 232–33; Ira Rutkow, *James A. Garfield* (New York: Holt, 2006), 11.

17. Geraldine Joncich Clifford, "Man/Woman/Teacher: Gender, Family, and Career in American Educational History," in *American Teachers: Histories of a Profession at Work*, ed. Donald Warren (New York: Macmillan, 1990), 294; Henke, "Preface," x–xi; Karen Benjamin, "The Decision to Teach: The Challenges and Opportunities of a One-Room School Teacher in Turn-of-the-Century Texas," *Thresholds in Education* 27, nos. 1 and 2 (2001): 18, 27; *One-Teacher Schools Today*, 22.

18. Paul F. Taylor, *Memories of a Mountain Educator: From a One-Room Schoolhouse to a College Classroom* (Baltimore: PublishAmerica, 2004), 12; Clark, *My Century in History*, 26; Benjamin, "The Decision to Teach," 25; Johnson, *Old-Time Schools and School Books*, 104; Hal S. Barron, *Mixed Harvest: The Second Great Transformation in the Rural North, 1870–1930* (Chapel Hill: University of North Carolina Press, 1997), 66; *The Consolidated Rural School*, ed. Louis W. Rapeer (New York: Scribner's, 1920), 23; Richard Watson Cooper and Hermann Cooper, *The One-Teacher School in Delaware: A Study in Attendance* (Newark: University of Delaware Press, 1925), 52.

19. Kaestle, *Pillars of the Republic*, 17–18; Warren Burton, *The District School as It Was, by One Who Went to It*, ed. Clifton W. Johnson (New York: Crowell, 1897), 53–54; "Blame the Red Schoolhouse: Its Methods of Teaching Were Grotesque, a Commission Says," *Kansas City Star*, 10 February 1912; *The McGuffey Readers: Selections from the 1879 Edition*, ed. Elliott J. Gorn (New York: Bedford/St. Martin's, 1998), vii, 2–3.

20. *Country School Legacy*, 33, 35; Mary C. Carlson and Robert L. Carlson, "The Country School and the Americanization of Immigrants to North Dakota," in Henke and Albers, *Legacy of North Dakota's Country Schools*, 6; Robert A. Caro, *The Years of Lyndon Johnson: The Path to Power* (New York: Knopf, 1982), 69.

21. William H. Hamby, "A Year in a Country School," *World's Work* 26 (1913): 231–32.

22. Ellis Ford Hartford, *The Little White Schoolhouse* (Lexington: University of Kentucky Press, 1977), 53; Chester Clark, "Memories," *Fowlersville*

(Michigan) *News and Views*, 14 February 1994, "Bowens Mills-Beyers" binder, Bess Britton Michigan One-Room Schoolhouse Collection, Van Buren District Library, Decatur, Michigan; Grove, *Legacy of One-Room Schools*, 66–68; Herbert A. Ellison, *The Old One-Room Country School* (Aurora, Colo.: National Writers Press, 1996), 9–10, 17, 13–14; Thomas, *Second Home*, 81.

23. Eric Sloane, *The Little Red Schoolhouse* (Garden City, N.Y.: Doubleday, 1972), 32; Thomas, *Second Home*, 75; Johnson, *Country School in New England*, 47; William V. Burgess, "Nostalgia in the Bicentennial Year," *Today's Education*, September–October 1976, p. 26, folder 2, box 1, One Room School House Association Collection, Special Collections, Penfield Library, State University of New York, Oswego; Johnson, *Old-Time Schools and School Books*, 123; Bobbie Kalman, *Historic Communities: The One-Room School* (New York: Crabtree, 1994), 25; Guinevere Koppler, "Crime and Punishment," in Tate and Tate, *Good Old Days Remembers*, 131; *My Folks and the One-Room Schoolhouse*, 57.

24. Hartford, *Little White Schoolhouse*, 58; Thomas, *Second Home*, 58; Koppler, "Crime and Punishment," 132; Johnson, *Country School in New England*, 51; Vinal, *Rise and Fall of Ye District School*, 57; Theobald, *Call School*, 137.

25. Burton, *District School as It Was*, 116–18; Richard Allen Foster, *The School in American Literature* (Baltimore: Warwick and York, 1930), 103; Perry, *Boyhood Days of Our Presidents*, 79; *Bulloch County One-Room Schools: A Walk Through Time* (Statesboro, Ga.: Bulloch County Historical Society, n.d. [2001]), 54; Otto L. Bettmann, *The Good Old Days—They Were Terrible!* (New York: Random House, 1974), 158; *One Room Country Schools: South Dakota Stories*, ed. Norma C. Wilson and Charles L. Woodard (Brookings: South Dakota Humanities Foundation, 1998), 81–82; Milt Riske, "Teacher's Gift," in Tate and Tate, *Good Old Days Remembers*, 52; Thomas, *Second Home*, 81; James L. Leloudis, *Schooling the New South: Pedagogy, Self, and Society in North Carolina, 1880–1920* (Chapel Hill: University of North Carolina Press, 1996), 17.

26. George F. Brown, "The Wondrous Tale of Little Man in Gosling Green," *New-Hampshire Gazette* (Portsmouth), 16 December 1834; *The Empty Schoolhouse: Memories of One-Room Texas Schools* (College Station: Texas A&M University Press, 1997), xiii; Marshall A. Barber, *The Schoolhouse at Prairie View* (Lawrence: University Press of Kansas, 1953), 61, 64; Edgar Logan, "Salute to the Little Red Schoolhouse," *Clearing House*

34 (October 1959): 78; *My Folks and the One-Room Schoolhouse*, iv; *Country School Legacy*, 38; Mary C. Carlson and Robert L. Carlson, "Rural Schools as Community Centers in North Dakota," in Henke and Albers, *Legacy of North Dakota's Country Schools*, 31; Fuller, *Old Country School*, 212; Wilson and Woodard, *One Room Country Schools: South Dakota Stories*, 115.

27. H. L. Mencken, *The American Language*, supp. 2 (1948; New York: Knopf, 1960), 304; Harriet Elinor Smith and Michael B. Frank, "Mark Twain's 'Spelling Match' Speech," *Southern Quarterly* 41 (Fall 2002): 5–9; Burton, *District School as It Was*, 56–57; Larry Beason, *Eyes Before Ease: The Unsolved Mysteries and Secret Histories of Spelling* (New York: McGraw-Hill, 2007), 48.

28. Ellen Litwicki, *America's Public Holidays, 1865–1920* (Washington, D.C.: Smithsonian Institution Press, 2000), 177–79; Fern Small, "The Passing of Gliddenburg School" (ms, n.d. [1993]), "Gliddenburg-Grubtown" binder; Helen Wiegmink to Bess Britton, n.d. [1993], "Volume A" binder; "78-Year-Old Recalls Life in One-Room Schoolhouse," *Muskegeon Chronicle*, 19 December 1999, "L" binder, all in Britton Collection.

29. *Country School Legacy*, 37–39; Robert L. Leigh and Alice Duffy Rinehart, *Country School Memories: An Oral History of One-Room Schooling* (Westport, Conn.: Greenwood, 1999), 2; *Bulloch County One-Room Schools*, 57; Grove, *Legacy of One-Room Schools*, 38; Swanson, *Rural One-Room Schools*, 10; Hartford, *Little White Schoolhouse*, 86, 78–79; *My Folks and the One-Room Schoolhouse*, 10; Helen Squiers, "Jessie School," *Slate* 11, no. 2 (Fall 2004): 2, "Slate" binder, Britton Collection; Tricia Crisafulli, "One-Room Schools Gone: How About the 3 R's?" *Palladium-Times* (Oswego, N.Y.), 11 March 1978, box 1, folder 7, One Room School House Association Collection.

30. Lenard E. Brown and Renzo Riddo, *Historic Structure Report: Freeman School, Homestead National Monument, Nebraska* (Denver, Colo.: Historic Preservation Team, National Park Service, 1973), pp. 4, 9–10, folder 12, box 10, Country School Legacy Collection; Clegg, *Empty Schoolhouse*, 174.

31. See Sister Nora Luetmer, "The History of Catholic Education in the Present Diocese of St. Cloud, Minnesota, 1885–1965" (Ph.D. diss., University of Minnesota, 1970). Thanks to Kathleen Conzen for calling my attention to this source. Carlson and Carlson, "Country School and the Americanization of Immigrants," 4–6; Theobold, *Call School*, 157.

32. Carlson and Carlson, "Country School and the Americanization of Immigrants," 6, 14; *Country School Legacy*, 33.

33. Hartford, *Little White Schoolhouse*, 59; Thomas, *Second Home*, 57–58; John Mack Faragher, *Sugar Creek: Life on the Illinois Prairie* (New Haven: Yale University Press, 1986), 122; Clark, *My Century in History*, 26.

34. Theobald, *Call School*, 88, 71–72; Johnson, *Old-Time Schools and School Books*, 102; Fuller, *Old Country School*, 60–61; John R. Stilgoe, *The Common Landscape of America, 1580 to 1845* (New Haven: Yale University Press, 1982), 244–45; Gulliford, *America's Country Schools*, 163; Henke, "Preface," xi.

35. Fred Kaplan, *The Singular Mark Twain: A Life* (New York: Doubleday, 2003), 29; Horace Mann, "Tenth Annual Report of the Secretary of the Massachusetts State Board of Education" (1846), at http://www.skidmore.edu/~tkuroda/hi323/mann.htm; *Henry Barnard's School Architecture*, ed. Jean McClintock and Robert McClintock (New York: Teachers College Press, 1970), 23; Alanson Halley to Henry Barnard, 24 February 1846, "Monroe Notes on HB, 1846–1848" folder, series 3, Barnard Papers.

36. Maud Barnett, *The School Beautiful* (Madison: Democrat Printing, 1907), 10; Leloudis, *Schooling the New South*, 156 (emphasis mine); Fletcher B. Dresslar, "The Construction and Care of School Buildings" (ms, n.d. [1913]), pp. 9–10, folder 15, box 9, Fletcher B. Dresslar Papers, Special Collections, Vanderbilt University, Nashville, Tenn.; "The Side Table: Editorial Sketches on Varied Minor Subjects," *Charlotte Observer*, 11 August 1913; Mary S. Hoffschwelle, *Rebuilding the Rural Southern Community: Reformers, Schools, and Homes in Tennessee, 1900–1930* (Knoxville: University of Tennessee, 1998), 24; Tracy L. Steffes, "A New Education for a Modern Age: National Reform, State-Building, and the Transformation of American Schooling, 1890–1933" (Ph.D. diss., University of Chicago, 2007), 147–48; J. L. Graham, "What Is the Function of the State in School-Building Programs?" *National Council on Schoolhouse Construction. Proceedings Eighth Annual Meeting* (Milwaukee: National Council on Schoolhouse Construction, n.d. [1930]), 21–22; *School Architecture: A Handy Manual for the Use of Architects and School Authorities*, ed. William G. Bruce (Milwaukee: American School Board Journal, 1910), 209–14, 237.

37. L. S. Mills, "The Little Red Schoolhouse," *American School Board Journal* 71 (October 1925): 53; Barron, *Mixed Harvest*, 65, 74; Donald Kraybill,

The Riddle of Amish Culture (Baltimore: Johns Hopkins University Press, 1989), 120; Steffes, "New Education for a Modern Age," 114; "Centralization of Schools," *Charlotte Observer,* 11 October 1910; Samuel T. Dutton and David S. Snedden, *The Administration of Public Education in the United States* (New York: Macmillan, 1908), 172; Philip Sumner Spence, "School Children in City Healthier Than in the Country," *New York Times,* 8 March 1914; "The Rural Department's Platform," *Journal of Rural Education* 1 (September 1921): 41–42.

38. Steffes, "New Education for a Modern Age," 16; Ben Walsh, "It Wasn't All Bad," in Henke and Albers, *Legacy of North Dakota's Country Schools,* 233; *Bulletin of the First District Normal School* 10 (June 1910): 108, Model Rural School Materials, Special Collections, Pickler Memorial Library, Truman State University, Kirksville, Missouri; Corey T. Lesseig, *Automobility: Social Changes in the American South, 1909–1939* (New York: Routledge, 2001), 77; "Brittain Speaks at Texas Meeting," *Atlanta Constitution,* 2 December 1911.

39. Edward Janak, "'Caught in a Tangled Skein': The Great Depression in South Carolina's Schools," in *Education and the Great Depression: Lessons from a Global History,* ed. E. Thomas Ewing and David Hicks (New York: Lang, 2006), 146; Lesseig, *Automobility,* 80; *Bulloch County One-Room Schools,* 34, 51; "More Schools and Better Ones," *Atlanta Independent,* 23 July 1914, reel 2, frame 759, Tuskegee Institute News Clipping File (Tuskegee, Ala.: Tuskegee Institute, 1978); Arthur Raper, *White and Negro Schools* (n.p.: National Association for the Advancement of Colored People, 1937), pp. 306, 319, fiche 001-543-1, Schomburg Center Clipping File, Schomburg Center for Research in Black Culture, New York Public Library.

40. Mary F. Hoffschwelle, *The Rosenwald Schools of the American South* (Gainesville: University of Florida Press, 2006), xii, 1, 136, 129; "Some of Mr. Rosenwald's Thoughts About Rural School Buildings" (ms, n.d. [1917]), p. 1, folder 1, box 331; "A General Statement of the Work of the Julius Rosenwald Fund in the South" (ms, n.d. [1922]), p. 2, folder 1, box 331; "Some Activities of the Julius Rosenwald Fund in the South" (ms, 1929), folder 2, box 331; Ruth Lockman to James F. Simon, 5 November 1934, folder 4, box 338, all in Julius Rosenwald Fund Archives, Special Collections, Fisk University, Nashville, Tennessee.

41. Alabama State Teachers' Association, *A Year Book on Negro Education in Alabama in 1930–31* (n.p., 1931), p. 32, fiche 001-528-1; "Georgia Edu-

cation" (ms, 1937), p. 3, fiche 001-543-1, both in Schomburg Center Clipping File; Adam Fairclough, *A Class of Their Own: Black Teachers in the Segregated South* (Cambridge: Harvard University Press, 2007), 297–98; E. P. Moon to Edward R. Embree, 27 November 1934, folder 3, box 331, Rosenwald Fund Archives; "Jackie Robinson," *New York Post*, 25 November 1959, fiche 003-459-1, Schomburg Center Clipping File.

42. "Struggles of His Youth Recalled by Latin Bishop," *Los Angeles Times*, 29 March 1970; Mary Melcher, "'This Is Not Right': Rural Arizona Women Challenge Segregation and Ethnic Division, 1925–1950," *Frontiers: A Journal of Women's Studies* 20, no. 2 (1999): 193; Peggy McCracken, "Museum Room Given Donation by Calderons," *Pecos Enterprise*, 24 December 1996, at http://www.pecos.net/news/archives/122496p.htm, accessed 7 February 2008; Eulalia Bourne, *Nine Months Is a Year at Baboquivari School* (Tuscon: University of Arizona Press, 1968), 72–73, 10.

T W O

Sentiment and Its Critics

1. "Red School House," *Omaha World-Herald*, 6 November 1892.
2. Levi Seeley, *A New School Management* (New York: Hinds and Noble, 1903), 60.
3. See, e.g., Richard Hofstadter, *The Age of Reform* (New York: Vintage, 1955), 23–24; David I. Macleod, *Building Character in the American Boy: The Boy Scouts, YMCA, and Their Forerunners, 1870–1920* (Madison: University of Wisconsin Press, 1983), 58–59; Edward J. Ward, *The Social Center* (New York: Appleton, 1915), 97; Ward, "The Little Red School House," *The Survey* 22 (7 August 1909): 640.
4. Walter S. Gedney, "The Little Red School House, Its Traditions and Fate," *Little Red Schoolhouse* 1, no.3 (January 1928), 1, 6.
5. John Greenleaf Whittier, "In School Days" (1870), in *An American Anthology, 1787–1900*, ed. Edmund Clarence Stedman (Boston: Houghton Mifflin, 1900), poem no. 223; Oliver Wendell Holmes to Whittier, 15 March 1870, in *The Letters of John Greenleaf Whittier*, ed. John B. Pickard (Cambridge: Belknap, 1975), 204.
6. Samuel T. Pickard, *Life and Letters of John Greenleaf Whittier*, 2 vols. (1907; New York: Haskell House, 1969), 2:545; Pickard, *Whittier-Land: A Handbook of North Essex* (1904; New York: Haskell House, 1973), 32.
7. James MacDougal Hart, *The Old School House* (Albany, 1849), reprod. in

Magazine *Antiques* (October 1998): 375; Claire Perry, *Young America: Childhood in Nineteenth-Century Art and Culture* (New Haven: Yale University Press, 2006), 186–87; Royall Tyler, *The Algerian Captive* (Gainesville: Scholars' Facsimile and Reprints, 1967); Walt Whitman, "Death in the School Room (A FACT)" (1841) at http://www.schooltales.net/death_schoolroom/; Daniel Pierce Thompson, *Locke Amsden; or, The Schoolmaster: A Tale* (Boston: Benjamin B. Mussey, 1852); Washington Irving, *The Legend of Sleepy Hollow* (New York: Tor Classics, 1991); Daniel Hoffman, "The Legend of Sleepy Hollow," in *Washington Irving: The Critical Reaction*, ed. James W. Tuttleton (New York: AMS Press, 1993), 92.

8. George F. Brown, "The Wondrous Tale of Little Man in Gosling Green," *New-Hampshire Gazette* (Portsmouth), 16 December 1834; "The Last of the Bodkins," *Yale Literary Magazine* 8 (1843): 308; "The Old Gambrel Roof," *Knickerbocker; or, New York Monthly Magazine* 52 (1858): 473.

9. "The Little Red Schoolhouse," *Boston Evening Transcript*, 17 January 1873, quoted in Nicolai Cikovsky, Jr., "Winslow Homer's *School Time:* 'A Picture Thoroughly National,'" in *In Honor of Paul Mellon*, ed. John Wilmerding (Washington, D.C.: National Gallery of Art, 1986), 48; Peter Fishe Reed, "The Old School-House," in Reed, *The Voices of the Wind, and Other Poems* (Chicago: E. B. Myers and Chandler, 1868), 172–76; Whittier, "In School Days."

10. Marjorie M. Hinds, "The Lure of a Vanished Life," *Elks Magazine* (May 1982): p. 17, folder 31, box 9, Country School Legacy Collection, University Archives, University of Colorado at Boulder Libraries; Arthur G. Burton, "Childhood," *New York Times*, 2 July 1902; T. S. Denison, *The Old Schoolhouse and Other Poems and Conceits in Verse* (Chicago: T. S. Denison, 1902), 11–14; Sue Thomas, *A Second Home: Missouri's Early Schools* (Columbia: University of Missouri Press, 2006), 75.

11. Whitman, "Death in the School Room"; Leslie A. Fiedler, *Love and Death in the American Novel* (New York: Criterion, 1960), 267–68; Marcia Jacobson, *Being a Boy Again: Autobiography and the American Boy Book* (Tuscaloosa: University of Alabama Press, 1994), 7–8; Glenn Hendler, *Public Sentiments: Structures of Feeling in Nineteenth-Century American Literature* (Chapel Hill: University of North Carolina Press, 2001), 190–91; George W. Peck, *Peck's Bad Boy and His Pa* (1883), quoted in Gail Schmunk Murray, *American Children's Literature and the Construction of Childhood* (New York: Twayne, 1998), 74.

12. Mark Twain, *The Adventures of Tom Sawyer* (New York: Oxford University Press, 1996), 70, 167, 174; William Dean Howells, *A Boy's Town: Described for "Harper's Young People"* (New York: Harper and Brothers, 1902), 60, 67.

13. Edward Eggleston, *The Hoosier School-Master*, ed. B. Edward McClellan (Bloomington: Indiana University Press, 1984), 5, 2; Eggleston, *The Hoosier Schoolmaster: A Story of Backwoods Life in Indiana*, rev. ed. (New York: Grosset and Dunlap, 1899), 15, 24.

14. Andrew Gulliford, *America's Country Schools*, 3rd ed. (Boulder: University Press of Colorado, 1996), 158; Cikovsky, "Winslow Homer's *School Time*," 47–48; Perry, *Young America*, 183; 1872 review of Winslow Homer's school series quoted in Margaret C. Conrads, *Winslow Homer and the Critics: Forging a National Art in the 1870s* (Princeton: Princeton University Press, 2001), 40; Elizabeth Johns, *Winslow Homer: The Nature of Observation* (Berkeley: University of California Press, 2002), 69–70.

15. *Will D. Cobb's School Days (When We Were a Couple of Kids)* (New York: Gus Edwards Publishing, 1906 and 1907), "Introduction: General History and Non-Michigan Schools" binder, Bess Britton Michigan One-Room Schoolhouse Collection, Van Buren District Library, Decatur, Michigan; Sigmund Spaeth, "The First Ten Since 1900," *New York Times*, 20 March 1949; "Gus Edwards," in *The Encyclopedia of Vaudeville*, ed. Anthony Slide (Westport, Conn.: Greenwood, 1994), 155–58; Richard Allen Foster, *The School in American Literature* (Baltimore: Warwick and York, 1930), 23.

16. Advertisement for *A Minister's Sweetheart*, *Atlanta Constitution*, 15 January 1911; "Amusements: Musical Comedy," *Atlanta Constitution*, 26 January 1925; *The School Teacher and the Waif*, dir. D. W. Griffith (American Biograph Company, 1912); "Mary Pickford Is Dead at 86: 'America's Sweetheart' of Films," *New York Times*, 30 May 1979.

17. Francis J. Bellamy to E. H. Hobson, 31 May 1892, folder 4; *Evening Exercises: National Columbus Celebration of Malden, Friday, October 21, 7:30 P.M.* (n.p., n.d. [1892]), p. 4, folder 9, both in box 1, Francis Julius Bellamy Papers, Department of Rare Books and Special Collections, University of Rochester Library; "The School Debt," *Daily Olympian* (Olympia, Washington), 19 July 1895.

18. "School Begins," *Puck*, 25 January 1899; Jonathan Zimmerman, *Innocents Abroad: American Teachers in the American Century* (Cambridge: Harvard University Press, 2006), 220; "One Phase of Imperialism," *Literary Di-*

gest 23 (7 September 1901); "The Filipino's Bugaboo," *Judge*, 5 August 1899.

19. Patricia Hills, "Picturing Progress in the Era of Westward Expansion," in *The West as America: Reinterpreting Images of the Frontier, 1820–1920*, ed. William H. Truettner (Washington, D.C.: Smithsonian Institution Press, 1991), 130; Bryan F. Le Beau, *Currier and Ives: America Imagined* (Washington, D.C.: Smithsonian Institution Press, 2001), 121–22; "The American Policy," *Judge*, 20 April 1901, cover; W. T. Stead, *The Americanization of the World: The Trend of the Twentieth Century* (New York: Horace Markley, 1901), 385, 387; "Little Red Schoolhouse," *Dallas Morning News*, 5 March 1906.

20. William B. Freer, *The Philippine Experiences of an American Teacher* (New York: Scribner's, 1906), 224; "Valley City Normal," *Grand Forks Daily Herald*, 10 January 1909; "Soap the Civilizer," *Miami Herald*, 9 August 1915; "20 American Colleges Offer Aid to Mexicans," *New York Times*, 2 January 1921; "Calls Education China's First Need," *New York Times*, 14 October 1923.

21. Thomas Nast, "The American River Ganges," *Harper's Weekly* (September 1871); Nast, "The Good-for-Nothing in Miss Columbia's Public School," *Harper's Weekly* (November 1871); "The Session in the House," *New York Times*, 4 December 1894; "Rioting in East Boston," *New York Times*, 5 July 1895; *The Annual Register: A Review of Public Events at Home and Abroad for the Year 1895* (London: Longmans Green, 1896), 380; Donald L. Kinzer, *An Episode in Anti-Catholicism: The American Protective Association* (Seattle: University of Washington Press, 1964), 52.

22. "Baptists in Baltimore," *New York Times*, 19 July 1895; "A Float Used Recently in a Public Parade in the Realm of Illinois," *Kourier* 1 (February 1925): 32; "Klan in Long Island," *New York Times*, 13 June 1926; Bishop Alma White, *The Ku Klux Klan in Prophecy* (Zarephath, N.J.: Pillar of Fire, 1925), 77; *Kourier* (June 1932): cover, reprinted in John J. Appel and Selma Appel, "The Huddled Masses and the Little Red Schoolhouse," in *American Education and the European Immigrant, 1840–1940*, ed. Bernard J. Weiss (Urbana: University of Illinois Press, 1982), 28.

23. Wayne E. Fuller, *The Old Country School: The Story of Rural Education in the Middle West* (Chicago: University of Chicago Press, 1982), 59; Robert James Ulrich, *The Bennett Law of 1889: Education and Politics in Wisconsin* (1965; New York: Arno, 1980), 425, 428; Kinzer, *Episode in Anti-Catholicism*, 65.

24. "Demmies Are Uneasy," *Dallas Morning News*, 5 November 1895; Wayne E. Fuller, "The Country School in the American Mind," *Journal of American Culture* 7 (Spring–Summer 1984): 14; "The President on Education," *New York Times*, 5 July 1924; W. W. Christman, "Little Red Schoolhouse," *New York Times*, 20 January 1924; "Vetoes Coolidge 'Slogan,'" *New York Times*, 6 January 1924.

25. "A Word to Mothers," *Kansas City Star*, 30 September 1884; "At Holland's," *Kansas City Star*, 17 November 1885; "Friday Morning—Shoe Day," *Grand Forks Daily Herald*, 10 September 1897; Joseph Dixon Crucible Company, "The Little Red School House" (n.p., n.d. [1908]); Cleveland Seating Company, *School Supplies*, catalogue no. 20 (n.p., n.d. [1920?]), both in box 5, Schools and School Supplies Series, Romaine Trade Catalogue Collection, Special Collections, Davidson Library, University of California, Santa Barbara.

26. "'The Little Red School House' The Birthplace of All Advertising," *San Jose Mercury News*, 26 April 1917; "School Days Ahead," *Atlanta Constitution*, 30 August 1925; "School Days—School Girls," *Atlanta Constitution*, 10 September 1919.

27. Hal Barron, *Mixed Harvest: The Second Great Transformation in the Rural North, 1870–1930* (Chapel Hill: University of North Carolina Press, 1997), 72; "Upstate Farmers Fight Lure of the City," *New York Times*, 17 March 1926; Harold Waldstein Fought, *The American Rural School* (New York: Macmillan, 1910), 307–8.

28. Philip Sumner Spence, "School Children in City Healthier Than in Country," *New York Times*, 8 March 1914; "Blame the Red Schoolhouse: Its Methods of Teaching Were Grotesque, a Commission Says," *Kansas City Star*, 10 February 1912; "The Country Schoolhouse," *New York Times*, 14 July 1894; Andrew P. Hill, "'And the Truth Shall Set Ye Free!' Some Thoughts on the California Rural School Situation" (ms, n.d. [1925?]), p. 5, series 3, box 3, folder 22, Andrew P. Hill, Jr., Papers, Holt-Atherton Department of Special Collections, University of the Pacific, Stockton, California.

29. *Country School Legacy: Humanities on the Frontier* (Silt, Colo.: Country School Legacy, 1981), 46; Tracy L. Steffes, "A New Education for a Modern Age: National Reform, State-Building, and the Transformation of American Schooling, 1890–1933" (Ph.D. diss., University of Chicago, 2007), 112–13; E. A. Duke to S. L. Smith, 2 March 1923, folder 1, box 342, Julius Rosenwald Fund Archives, Special Collections, Fisk Univer-

sity, Nashville, Tennessee; "Seal on the Little Red School," *Aberdeen* (S.D.) *Daily News,* 17 August 1909; "Farmers as Businessmen," *New York Times,* 12 July 1912.

30. Richard Watson Cooper and Hermann Cooper, *The One-Room School in Delaware: A Study in Attendance* (Newark: University of Delaware Press, 1925), 30; L. S. Mills, "The Little Red Schoolhouse," *American School Board Journal* 71 (October 1925): 52–53.

31. John Bodnar, *Remaking America: Public Memory, Commemoration, and Patriotism in the Twentieth Century* (Princeton: Princeton University Press, 1992), 115–16; David Glassberg, *American Historical Pageantry: The Uses of Tradition in the Early Twentieth Century* (Chapel Hill: University of North Carolina Press, 1990), 270; "The Rural School Problem," *Delaware School News* 1 (March 1920): p. 2, file 712-47, box 1237, Pierre S. Du Pont Papers, Hagley Museum and Library, Wilmington, Delaware.

32. "The Little School House," *San Jose Mercury News,* 15 May 1907; "Preparing to Spend Millions on Moving Picture Shows," *San Jose Mercury News,* 10 July 1912.

33. George McAdam, "The Crisis in Our Schools," *World's Work* 40 (1920): 252; "Educator Scores 'Snob' Advice and Psychology Test," *Little Red Schoolhouse* 2 (December 1929): 2; "Rural Mother" in Barron, *Mixed Harvest,* 71; "Keep the Home Fires Burning," *Little Red Schoolhouse* 1 (August–September 1928): 2; "Bureaucracy Is the Worst Form of Tyranny," *Little Red Schoolhouse* 5 (November 1933): 3.

34. George E. Schuester, "Is Modern Education Detrimental?" *Little Red Schoolhouse* 1 (August–September 1928): 8; Jerome Judd, "Speech in Defense of Rural Schools," *Little Red Schoolhouse* 1 (May 1928): 7; John B. Weig, "A Plea to Parents," *Little Red Schoolhouse* 2 (February 1930): 3.

35. "W.W.C.," "The Little Red Schoolhouse," *New York Times,* 17 April 1927; Edna M. Hill, "The Little Red Schoolhouse a 'Fake,'" *Independent* (7 August 1913): 316; O'Shea, "Passing of the District School," 234.

36. *Country School Legacy,* 46; "Seldom Heard of Now: The 'Little Red Schoolhouse' No More a Political Issue," *New York Times,* 22 October 1916; James Quinten Cahill, "Herbert Hoover's Early Schooling in Iowa and Its Place in Presidential Politics, Community Memory, and Personal Identity," *Annals of Iowa* 61 (2002): 151–91; A. J. Ladd, "Improvements in Our Public Schools," *Grand Forks Daily Herald,* 29 January 1911; "'Who's Who' and the Little Red Schoolhouse," *Journal of Rural Education* 4 (November 1924): 135.

37. *One-Teacher Schools Today* (Washington, D.C.: Research Division, National Education Association, June 1960), 9; Corey T. Lesseig, *Automobility: Social Changes in the American South, 1909–1939* (New York: Routledge, 2001), 76–77; Foster Ware, "In Rural America the Picture Changes," *New York Times*, 24 July 1927; "Guilford County Will Erect Many New Schools," *Charlotte Observer*, 12 December 1922.

38. Ward, *Social Center*, 96, 102; Kevin Mattson, *Creating a Democratic Public: The Struggle for Urban Participatory Democracy During the Progressive Era* (University Park: Pennsylvania State University Press, 1998), 53–54, 67; Wayne E. Fuller, *One-Room Schools of the Middle West: An Illustrated History* (Lawrence: University Press of Kansas, 1994), 6; Josephus Daniels, "The Little Red Schoolhouse," *Fort Worth Star-Telegram*, 13 September 1912.

39. Zimmerman, *Innocents Abroad*, 24; Charles Everett Myers, "The One-Teacher School, Front and Center," *Journal of Rural Education* 3 (May–June 1924): 439–40; "Back to the District School," *New York Times*, 29 May 1926.

40. Dorothy Canfield Fisher, *Understood Betsy* (1916; New York: Holt, 1917), 101, 105; Ida H. Washington, *Dorothy Canfield Fisher: A Biography* (Shelburne, Vt.: New England Press, 1982), 69–70; *Keeping Fires Night and Day: Selected Letters of Dorothy Canfield Fisher*, ed. Mark J. Madigan (Columbia: University of Missouri Press, 1993), 19, 40n2; Dorothy Canfield Fisher, *Montessori for Parents* (1912; Cambridge, Mass.: Robert Bentley, 1965), 232.

41. Elizabeth Yates, *The Lady from Vermont: Dorothy Canfield Fisher's Life and World* (Brattleboro, Vt.: Stephen Greene Press, 1958), 115–16; Washington, *Dorothy Canfield Fisher*, 205; Dorothy Canfield Fisher, *Self-Reliance* (Indianapolis: Bobbs-Merrill, 1916), 233.

42. "Clara Barton: Teacher in New Jersey" (ms, n.d. [1920]), "Correspondence. Undated" folder; "Clara Barton Schoolhouse," *Education Bulletin*, October 1920, "Correspondence 1920" folder, both in box 1, Clara Barton Schoolhouse Fund Series, Commissioner's Office Subgroup, Department of Education Records, New Jersey State Archives, Trenton; "The Little Red Schoolhouse Finds a Home at Last: The Building at Woodbury, L.I.," *New York Times*, 6 March 1927; "Once Poor, Man Gives $400,000 for Nathan Hale Schoolhouse," *New York Times*, 17 February 1929.

43. *The Story of Mary and Her Little Lamb, as Told by Mary and Her Neighbors and Friends* (Dearborn, Mich.: Mr. and Mrs. Henry Ford, 1928), 2–4, 27; Ford

R. Bryan, *Beyond the Model T: The Other Ventures of Henry Ford* (Detroit: Wayne State University Press, 1990), 176; William Adams Simons, *Henry Ford and Greenfield Village* (New York: Frederick A. Stokes, 1938), 67.

44. Steven Watts, *The People's Tycoon: Henry Ford and the American Century* (New York: Vintage, 2005), 480–81; Bryan, *Beyond the Model T*, 181; Geoffrey C. Upward, *A Home for Our Heritage: The Building and Growth of Greenfield Village and Henry Ford Museum, 1929–1979* (Dearborn, Mich.: Henry Ford Museum Press, 1979), 23, 42; Simons, *Henry Ford and Greenfield Village*, 42.

45. Watts, *People's Tycoon*, 421–22; Thomas H. Reed, "Rural Local Governments Found Unequal to Burdens," *New York Times*, 24 January 1932; Firestone Truck and Rubber Company, *Consolidated Rural Schools and the Motor Truck*, Bulletin No. 6 (Akron: Firestone Ship by Truck Bureau, July 1920), p. 33, file 712-28, box 1226, du Pont Papers.

THREE

From Poverty to Democracy

1. John Vachon, "Stories of Groups of People" (ms, n.d. [1940]), reel NDA4, Roy E. Stryker Papers, American Archives of Art, Smithsonian Institution, Washington, D.C.; Marion Post Wolcott photograph, LC-USF34-05584-D; Wolcott photograph, LC-USF34-055907-D; Wolcott photograph, LC-USF34-055830-D, all in Farm Security Administration—Office of War Information Photograph Collection, Prints and Photographs Division, Library of Congress, Washington, D.C.

2. "Little Blue Schoolhouse," *New York Times*, 19 June 1955; "Little Red Schoolhouse," *Nation* (28 May 1955): 453; William Lee Miller, "Little Red Schoolhouse in the Middle of the Road," *Reporter* (20 October 1955): 32–36; Emilie Davie, *Profile of America: An Autobiography of the USA* (New York: Crowell, 1954), 307.

3. Hazen Chatfield, "Foreword," in *The Old Red School House of East Chester: The Story of Public School 15, the Bronx, and Its Historic Background* (n.p., 14 April 1942), "The Old Red Schoolhouse of Eastchester" folder, box 5, Little Red Schoolhouse Collection, Special Collections, Lehman College Library, the Bronx, New York; Sue Thomas, *A Second Home: Missouri's Early Schools* (Columbia: University of Missouri Press, 2006), 132.

4. *One-Teacher Schools Today* (Washington, D.C.: Research Division, National Education Association, June 1960), 9; "Topics of the Times," *New*

York Times, 3 April 1956; Margaret Mead, *The School in American Culture* (Cambridge: Harvard University Press, 1951), 7, 9.

5. "Roosevelt Hailed as 1932 President," *New York Times*, 5 December 1928.

6. Warren A. Henke, "Teachers: Their Roles, Rules, and Restrictions," in *The Legacy of North Dakota's Country Schools*, ed. Warren A. Henke and Everett C. Albers (Bismarck: North Dakota Humanities Council, 1998), 115; "153,306 One-Teacher Schools Pay Average of $874 a Year," *New York Times*, 5 July 1931; "Says Nation Tends to Create Peasants," *New York Times*, 3 July 1931; Eunice Fuller Barnard, "Our Schools Face a Day of Reckoning," *New York Times*, 15 April 1934.

7. Barnard, "Our Schools Face a Day of Reckoning"; "The Question of Federal Financial Aid for School Construction," *Congressional Digest* 36, no 11 (November 1957): p. 259, "S889" folder, box 32, Office Files of the Commissioner of Education, Office of Education Records, Record Group 12, National Archives 2, College Park, Maryland; N. E. Viles, "The National School Facilities Survey," *Indiana and Midwest School Building Planning Conference: Proceedings* (Bloomington: Division of Research and Field Services, Indiana University, 1952), 35; S. L. Smith, "Progress in School Building Construction," *National Council on Schoolhouse Construction: Proceedings of the 17th Annual Meeting* (Milwaukee: National Council on Schoolhouse Construction, 1939), 24–25; Howard T. Herber, *The Influence of the Public Works Administration on School Building Construction in New York State, 1933–1936* (New York: Teachers College Press, 1938), 74; "Schoolhouses for Sale," *New York Times*, 19 September 1939.

8. David Tyack, Robert Lowe, and Elisabeth Hansot, *Public Schools in Hard Times: The Great Depression and Recent Years* (Cambridge: Harvard University Press, 1984), 106–7; Democratic National Campaign Committee, "What Happened to the Little Red Schoolhouse?" (n.p., 1936), Hay Broadsides Collection, John Hay Library, Brown University, Providence, Rhode Island.

9. Eugene F. Provenzo, Jr., "One-Room and Country Schools Depicted in Farm Security Administration Photographs," in *Education and the Great Depression: Lessons from a Global History*, ed. E. Thomas Ewing and David Hicks (New York: Peter Lang, 2006), 177–80; "Mrs. Marion Wolcott" (ms, n.d.), reel NDA4, Stryker Papers; Marion Post Wolcott interview, 18 January 1965 (ms, 18 January 1965), 5, Oral History Collection, Archives of American Art; *A Kentucky Album: Farm Security Administra-*

tion Photographs, 1935–1943, ed. Beverly W. Brannan and David Horvath (Lexington: University Press of Kentucky, 1986), 54.

10. Russell Lee photograph, LC-USF34-030798-D; Lee photograph, LC-USF34-032901-D; Lee photograph, LC-USF34-070543-D; Marion Post Wolcott photograph, LC-USF34-056128-D; Wolcott photograph, LC-USF34-055907-D, all in Farm Security Administration—Office of War Information Photograph Collection; Brannan and Horvath, *Kentucky Album*, 62.

11. Russell Lee photograph, LC-USF34-035090-D; Lee photograph, LC-USF34-035086-D; John Collier photograph, LC-USW3-014511-E; Collier photograph, LC-USW3-01472-C, all in Farm Security Administration—Office of War Information Photograph Collection.

12. Marion Wolcott photograph, LC-USF34-055830-D, in Farm Security Administration—Office of War Information Photograph Collection; Melissa A. McEuen, *Seeing America: Women Photographers Between the Wars* (Lexington: University Press of Kentucky, 2000), 175; John Vachon photograph, LC-USF34-064712-D; Russell Lee photograph, LC-USF33-011605-M2; Lee photograph, LC-USF34-010981-E; Arthur Rothstein photograph, LC-USF34-028414-D; Marion Post Wolcott photograph, LC-USF34-055721-D, all in Farm Security Administration—Office of War Information Photograph Collection; "General caption No. 24. A Pie Supper in Muskogee County, Oklahoma" (ms, n.d. [1940?]), frames 573–75, reel FSA/WDC1, Farm Security Administration Photography Project Records, Archives of American Art; James Agee, *Let Us Now Praise Famous Men* (New York: Library of America, 2005), 258, 357.

13. David Glassberg, *American Historical Pageantry: The Uses of Tradition in the Early Twentieth Century* (Chapel Hill: University of North Carolina Press, 1990), 271–72; John Bodnar, *Remaking America: Public Memory, Commemoration, and Patriotism in the Twentieth Century* (Princeton: Princeton University Press, 1992), 128; Margaret L. Baker to Department of Education, 22 April 1930, "Correspondence 1930" folder, box 1, Clara Barton Schoolhouse Fund Series, Commissioner's Office Subgroup, Department of Education Records, New Jersey State Archives, Trenton; Elizabeth M. Thompson, "Commencement at Norwich High School," *English Journal* 26 (March 1937): 199–204; Helen Yuhasz, "The Development of Public Lands and Colonial Policies in America and Our Debt to the Ordinance of 1787" (ms, n.d. [1937]), "Essays" folder, box

16, Northwest Territory Celebration Commission Records, Record Group 148, National Archives 2.

14. Carol Ryrie Brink, *Caddie Woodlawn* (New York: Aladdin, 1990); Brink, "'Caddie Woodlawn': Newbery Medal Winner 1936: Her History," *Horn Book* 12 (July 1936): 250.

15. John E. Miller, *Becoming Laura Ingalls Wilder: The Woman Behind the Legend* (Columbia: University of Missouri Press, 1998), 3, 181–83; Laura Ingalls Wilder, *On the Banks of Plum Creek* (New York: HarperCollins, 2004); Wilder, *Little Town on the Prairie* (New York: HarperCollins, 2004), 273–74; Ann Romines, *Constructing the Little House: Gender, Culture, and Laura Ingalls Wilder* (Amherst: University of Massachusetts Press, 1997), 201–2.

16. Virginia L. Wolf, *Little House on the Prairie: A Reader's Companion* (New York: Twayne, 1996), 110–15; Romines, *Constructing the Little House*, 216; Laura Ingalls Wilder, *These Happy Golden Years* (New York: HarperCollins, 2004), 139, 153.

17. David Weaver-Zercher, *The Amish in the American Imagination* (Baltimore: Johns Hopkins University Press, 2001), 61, 214n35, 67, 69–70; "New Amish School Strike Looms in Pennsylvania," *New York Times*, 5 September 1938.

18. Esther Gray, "Modern Ideas Enter Our Public Schools," *New York Times*, 1 June 1930; Agnes De Lima, *The Little Red School House* (New York: Macmillan, 1948), 207; Sol Cohen, *Progressives and Urban School Reform: The Public Education Association of New York City, 1895–1954* (New York: Teachers College Press, 1963), 123, 132–34; Caroline F. Ware, *Greenwich Village, 1920–1930* (1935; New York: Octagon, 1977), 343–44; "New and Old Clash at Public School 41," *New York Times*, 1 May 1932; "Says 'Little School' Lags in Its Results," *New York Times*, 7 May 1932; "The Experimental School," *New York Times*, 13 May 1932.

19. David A. Elms, "'Progressivism' in Schools," *New York Times*, 9 March 1937; R. E. Prescott, "The Little Brown School," *Detroit Saturday Night*, 31 August 1933; H. L. Mencken, "Schoolhouses in the Red," *Little Red Schoolhouse* 5 (October–November 1934): 1, 4. Thanks to Jeffrey Mirel for calling my attention to the Detroit reference.

20. Darrell Garwood, *Artists in Iowa: A Life of Grant Wood* (1944; Westport, Conn.: Greenwood, 1971), 139–41; James M. Dennis, *Grant Wood: A Study in American Art and Culture* (Columbia: University of Missouri Press, 1986), 219; "Such Is Life," *Life* (March 1935): 52.

Notes to Pages 115–21

21. "Pittsfield Sees Art in Our Crazy Times," *Art Digest* 13 (1 September 1939): 12; Don L. Goddard, *Tschacbasov* (New York: American Archives of World Art, 1964), 23.

22. Committee on Rural Education, *Still Sits the Schoolhouse by the Road* (Chicago: Committee on Rural Education, 1943), 121; *The White House Conference on Rural Education* (Washington, D.C.: National Education Association, 1945), 30–31, 116; "The Little Red Schoolhouse," *New York Times*, 5 October 1944.

23. Chatfield, "Foreword," in *Old Red School House;* "They Builded Better Than They Knew," *New York Times*, 30 June 1944.

24. Iman Elise Schatzmann, *The Country School at Home and Abroad* (Chicago: University of Chicago Press, 1942), vii, xi; "Germans Capitulate on All Fronts," *New York Times*, 8 May 1945; Fred E. H. Schroeder, "The Little Red Schoolhouse," in *Icons of America*, ed. Ray B. Browne and Marshall Fishwick (Bowling Green, Ky.: Popular Press, 1978), 139; W. G. Vorpe, "As the Parade Passes By," *Cleveland Plain Dealer*, 20 May 1945, folder 6, box 11, Country School Legacy Collection, University Archives, University of Colorado at Boulder Libraries.

25. Leslie C. Swanson, *Rural One-Room Schools of Mid-America* (Moline, Ill.: Leslie Swanson, 1976), 31; "Red Schoolhouses Dwindle," *New York Times*, 19 February 1955; Jennie D. Lindquist, "A Tribute to Laura Ingalls Wilder," *Horn Book* 29 (December 1953): 411; Jonathan Zimmerman, *Whose America? Culture Wars in the Public Schools* (Cambridge: Harvard University Press, 2002), 91.

26. Seymour Freidin and William Richardson, "Free at Last from the Little Red Schoolhouse," *Colliers* (25 December 1953): 106–8; "The 'Hate America' Campaign," *New York Times*, 5 October 1952; "New 'Little Red Schoolhouse,'" *New York Times*, 16 September 1954; "Tower Ticker," *Chicago Tribune*, 29 March 1949; E. M. Root, *How Red Is the Little Red Schoolhouse?* (Chicago: M.A. Pennington, 1953), item 2205, Donner Shelved Holdings, Robert Donner Collection, Brown Library, Abilene Christian University, Abilene, Texas.

27. L. D. Warren, "It was against the rule," 21 May 1954; Warren, "Not so fast! You're supposed to follow me," n.d., both in Cartoon Research Library, Ohio State University Libraries, Columbus, Ohio; Bill Mauldin, "What is done in our classrooms today will be reflected in the successes or failures of civilization tomorrow," *Saint Louis Post-Dispatch*, 11 November 1958, Bill Mauldin Papers, Library of Congress, Washington, D.C.

28. "School Shortage Plagues Suffolk," *New York Times*, 11 November 1956; "Emergency Classrooms," *Washington Post*, 16 November 1956, both in "School Con., Sup. Materials, Classroom Needs 1956 and 1957" folder, box 81, School Construction Assistance Papers, Office of Education Records; Frank P. Schroeter to Fall River Board of Trustees, 8 September 1954, folder 3752: 1729, Department of Education Records, California State Archives, Sacramento; "Race with the Stork" (1954); L. D. Warren, "He's through as soon as he starts!" 5 September 1956, both in Cartoon Research Library; "Money Problems and Crowded Schools," *New York Times*, 15 February 1959.

29. Henry Roth, "One Room School" (ms, October 1947), p. 1, folder 11, box 37; Roth, "Schoolhouse Recollections" (ms, n.d. [1948]), pp. 8–9, folder 8, box 38, both in Henry Roth Papers, Center for Jewish History, New York.

30. John Steinbeck, *East of Eden* (New York: Viking, 1952), 147; Mrs. James S. Ayars [Rebecca Caudill] to Nancy E. Valtin, 9 May 1949, folder 1, box 7, Rebecca Caudill Papers, Special Collections, Margaret I. King Library, University of Kentucky, Lexington; Edgar Logan, "Salute to the Little Red Schoolhouse," *Clearing House* 34 (October 1959): 78.

31. Wayne E. Fuller, *One-Room Schools of the Middle West: An Illustrated History* (Lawrence: University Press of Kansas, 1994), 123–24; "Farewell Party on Staten Island Marks Closing of 46-Year-Old Rural School," *New York Times*, 1 July 1943; Robert L. Leigh and Alice Duffy Rinehart, *Country School Memories: An Oral History of One-Room Schooling* (Westport, Conn.: Greenwood, 1999), inset.

32. Fuller, *One-Room Schools of the Middle West*, 125–29; Swanson, *Rural One-Room Schools of Mid-America*, 4; Jerry Apps, *One-Room Country Schools: History and Recollections from Wisconsin* (Amherst, Wisc.: Amherst Press, 1996), 184; "Schoolhouses for Sale," *New York Times*, 19 September 1939; "The Corner Shop at Macy's," *New York Times*, 15 September 1943.

33. Hotel Bader advertisement, *New York Times*, 19 May 1957, p. X36; B. Altman and Company advertisement, *New York Times*, 9 March 1958, p. 76; "Shop Talk: Store in Bid to Lure Career Girls," *New York Times*, 26 August 1958; "See What's Ticking for Christmas at Gimbels," *New York Times*, 6 December 1964, p. 65; "Parker Games Are Family Games," *New York Times*, 7 December 1952, p. 75; "Everybody's Happy Playing Famous Parker Games," *New York Times*, 13 December 1953, p. SM67; *Little Red School House Game* (Salem, Mass.: Parker Brothers, 1952).

34. "Topics of the Times," *New York Times*, 3 April 1956; Horace Seeley-Brown, Jr., to William D. Hassett, 28 April 1952; Harry S. Truman to Seeley-Brown, enclosed with David D. Lloyd to Mabel Williams, 19 May 1952, both in President's Personal File no. 6053, Harry S. Truman Library, Independence, Missouri; Dwight D. Eisenhower to Horace Seeley-Brown, Jr., 19 May 1954, "PPF 22-C Quasset School, Woodstock, Connecticut," folder, box 681, President's Personal Files, White House Central Files, Dwight D. Eisenhower Library, Abilene, Kansas; "1748 Schoolhouse Becomes a Shrine," *New York Times*, 25 May 1954; "25th Debut Planned for First School," *Oberlin News-Tribune*, 25 September 1958, Oberlin Little Red Schoolhouse Subject File, Oberlin College Archives, Oberlin, Ohio; "One-Room School Is Restored in New Canaan," *New York Times*, 3 December 1962.

35. Steven Watts, *The People's Tycoon: Henry Ford and the American Century* (New York: Vintage, 2005), 414, 481; William Adam Simons, *Henry Ford and Greenfield Village* (New York: Frederick A. Stokes, 1938), 43, 63; Geoffrey C. Upward, *A Home for Our Heritage: The Building and Growth of Greenfield Village and Henry Ford Museum, 1929–1979* (Dearborn, Mich.: Ford Museum Press, 1979), 138–39; E. Lucile Webster, *An Autobiography of a One-Room School Teacher* (Dearborn, Mich.: E. Lucile Webster, 1978), 173.

36. Upward, *A Home for Our Heritage*, 146; "Schoolroom Progress USA!" *Chicago Defender*, 12 November 1958.

37. James A. Farley, "Tribute to Teachers," *New York Times*, 27 May 1956; William Gould Vinal, *The Rise and Fall of Ye District School in Plimouth Plantation (1800–1900)* (Norwell, Mass.: Vinehall, 1958), 177; Jonathan Zimmerman, *Innocents Abroad: American Teachers in the American Century* (Cambridge: Harvard University Press, 2006), 178.

38. Kitty Hanson, "City Still Has a Little Red Schoolhouse," *New York Daily News*, 22 January 1955; Nancyann Rella, "Childhood Memories Come Alive," *Daily Argus* (Mount Vernon, N.Y.), 25 January 1981, both in "Little Red Schoolhouse—Memoirs, Historical Articles" folder, box 5, Little Red Schoolhouse Collection.

FOUR

Open Classroom or Back to Basics?

1. "From Chicken Coop to Education Museum" *Outlook* (SUNY, Oswego), 1974, folder 7; Julia M. Warger, "Rural Education in the One-Room

Schoolhouse in America Since the Revolution" (ms, 11 December 1980), p. 10, folder 6, both in box 1, One Room School House Association Collection, Special Collections, Penfield Library, State University of New York, Oswego.

2. "Patriotism," *Palladium-Times* (Oswego, N.Y.), n.d. [1975], folder 7, box 1, One Room School House Association Collection.

3. "History of the President's Old Schoolhouse," *Herald Tribune*, 14 April 1965; "Johnson, at Old School, Signs Education Aid Bill," *Washington Post*, 12 April 1965, both in book 11, White House Social Office—Scrapbook, March–May 1965, Lyndon B. Johnson Library and Museum, Austin, Texas; Edwin C. Bearss, *Historic Structure: Junction School, Lyndon B. Johnson National Historic Site* (Denver, Colo.: Historic Preservation Team, National Park Service, May 1975), 49–50.

4. Richard Pankratz to Andrew Gulliford, 15 December 1982, folder 34, box 10, Country School Legacy Collection, University Archives, University of Colorado, Boulder; Christopher B. Manaseri, "Keeping School: One-Room Schoolhouse Preservation Projects in the Greater Finger Lakes Region of New York State" (Ph.D. diss., Syracuse University, 2004), 4; Oliver L. McAllister to Lyndon B. Johnson, n.d. [May 1966], "New Jersey" folder, box 1489, National Park Service Records, Record Group 79, National Archives 2, College Park, Maryland; Harry Martin, "Gliddenburg School" (ms, n.d. [1990?], "Gliddenburg-Grubtown" binder, Bess Britton Michigan One-Room Schoolhouse Collection, Van Buren District Library, Decatur, Michigan.

5. Manaseri, "Keeping School," 4; Elizabeth Brennan, "Down East Memory Lane: Maine's One-Room Schoolhouses Represent a Lost Way of Life," *Preservation Online*, 8 March 2002, at http://www.nationaltrust.org/magazine/archives/arch_story/030802.htm; Jane Doan, "Circling Back," in *Full Circle: A New Look at Multiage Education*, ed. Penelle Chase and Jane Doan (Portsmouth, N.H.: Heinemann, 1994), 3–4; Bruce Hammond, "Well, we've certainly come a long way," *Boston Globe*, 17 December 1997.

6. WRBG [Schenectady, N.Y.], "The Little Red Schoolhouse" (ms, n.d. [1964]), 2; "Two in a row," *Middleburgh* (N.Y.) *News*, n.d. [1964]; "See Little Red Schoolhouse," advertisement, n.p., n.d. [1964]; "Dave Kroman, TV Prof Interviewed at W.R.G.B.," *The Triune* (Catholic Central High School, Troy, N.Y.), 30 October 1964; "Schenectady General Electric Presents Berne-Knox Central vs. Schalmont Central in a Battle of

Brains on 'Little Red Schoolhouse,'" advertisement, n.p., n.d. [1964], all in folder 1, box 2, Martha Brooks Papers, National Public Broadcasting Archives, Hornbake Library, University of Maryland, College Park.

7. James N. Reston, "Are We Back to the Little Red Schoolhouse?" *Grade Teacher* 83 (February 1966): 108; "Nongrade School Both Old and New," *New York Times*, 21 November 1968, p. 38; "Look What Two Teachers Have Done in the Little Red Schoolhouse," *Grade Teacher* 82 (September 1964): 37.

8. Winthrop Griffith, "A Daring Educational Experiment," *New York Times*, 30 May 1971; Ben Logan, *The Land Remembers* (New York: Viking, 1975), 197; Frances C. Marbury, "The One-Room School: Once Essential, Still Ideal," *Middlebury News Letter* (Spring 1970), p. 18, Little Red Schoolhouse Collection, University Archives, Lehman Library, Shippensburg University, Shippensburg, Pennsylvania.

9. "One-Room School Is Resurrected," *SPL Reports*, September 1964, p. 5, folder 2850/4, box 1, School Planning Laboratory Papers, Special Collections and University Archives, Stanford University, Palo Alto, Calif.; Educational Facilities Laboratories, *Transformation of the Schoolhouse* (New York: Educational Facilities Laboratories, 1969), 8–9; "1-room School Rediscovered," *Christian Science Monitor*, 24 December 1973; Griffith, "Daring Educational Experiment."

10. "Nongrade School Both Old and New"; "Mrs. B.R.," "Give Us Back Our Children," *Chicago Defender*, 6 July 1970; Dwain Preston, "The Little Red Schoolhouse Revisited," *Illinois Quarterly* 35 (February 1973): pp. 16–19, folder 1, box 1, One Room School House Association Collection; David B. Tyack, "The Tribe and the Common School," *American Quarterly* 24 (March 1972): 17.

11. Ellis Ford Hartford, *The Little White Schoolhouse* (Lexington: University Press of Kentucky, 1977), 95, 97; *Readin' 'Ritin' 'Rithmetic and Reminiscin': A Bicentennial Project by the Iowa Retired Teachers Association* (n.p.: Iowa Retired Teachers Association, 1976), 79, 119.

12. Eric Sloane, *The Little Red Schoolhouse* (Garden City, N.Y.: Doubleday, 1972), 18; *Readin' 'Ritin' 'Rithmetic and Reminiscin'*, 147; Clennie Hollon to Ellis Ford Hartford, 7 November 1977, folder 5, box 136, Ellis Ford Hartford Papers, Manuscript and Folklife Archives, Kentucky Library and Museum, Western Kentucky University, Bowling Green.

13. "Archie: Showdown at the Little Red Schoolhouse," in *Archie's Parables* (n.p.: Spire Christian Comics, 1975).

14. Gary Libman, *Little House on the Prairie* (Mankato, Minn.: Creative Education, 1983), 11–12, 16; *Cat Ballou*, dir. Elliot Silverstein (Columbia Pictures Corporation, 1965); *Sara* (Columbia Broadcasting Company, 1976); *The Quick Gun*, dir. Sidney Salkow (Robert E. Kent Productions, 1964).

15. "Archie: Showdown at the Little Red Schoolhouse"; "Busing Protest Jams Traffic for 25 Miles," *Washington Post*, 18 February 1972.

16. John Hope Franklin, "Busing Trick to 'Protect' Bias," *Chicago Defender*, 14 September 1971; Roger S. Kuhn, "More Comment on the School Busing Issue and Mr. Nixon's Plan," *Washington Post*, 29 March 1972; Dennis Hathaway, "Busing and Integration Down on the Farm," *Los Angeles Times*, 14 June 1978.

17. James F. Hopkins, review of Ellis Ford Hartford, *The Little White Schoolhouse*, in *Register of the Kentucky Historical Society*, July 1978, folder 4, box 136, Hartford Papers; "Jersey Town Reviving History," *New York Times*, 11 July 1965; "Old Schoolhouse Still in Use," *New York Times*, 1 September 1974.

18. *One Room Country Schools: South Dakota Stories*, ed. Norma C. Wilson and Charles L. Woodard (Brookings: South Dakota Humanities Foundation, 1998), 136–37; "America the Beautiful Fund" (ms, n.d.), America the Beautiful Fund Headquarters, Washington, D.C.; *People's History Information Exchange* (n.p., n.d.; 1976), folder 21, box 1, One Room School House Association Collection.

19. *Readin' 'Ritin' 'Rithmetic and Reminiscin'*, 3, 186; Leslie C. Swanson, *Rural One-Room Schools of Mid-America* (Moline, Ill.: Leslie Swanson, 1976), 5; "Alumnus Fights for Landmark," *Bowling Green News*, 10 May 1974; "Big Lad Takes on Weighty Project," *Toledo Blade*, 8 February 1972, both in Little Red Schoolhouse folder, Center for Archival Collections, Bowling Green State University, Bowling Green, Ohio.

20. "Children Go from 20th to 19th Century for 3R's," *Syracuse Herald-Journal*, 24 October 1973; "Students Rough It at Historic Schoolhouse," newspaper clipping, n.p., 21 May 1975, both in folder 7, box 1, One Room School House Association Collection.

21. "Country School Legacy: NEH Project Documents Rural Education," *History News* 36 (April 1981): pp. 13–14, folder 1, box 1, One Room School House Association Collection; *Country School Legacy: Humanities on the Frontier* (Silt, Colo.: Country School Legacy, 1981), 4; Country School Legacy, "Seminar Sites, June 1981–July 1982" (ms, 1 August

1982), folder 13; Country School Legacy, "Troubleshooting the Seminars" (ms, n.d. [1981]), folder 8; Sandy Scofield to Andrew Gulliford, 14 July 1981, folder 16; Cleda Davis, "Seminar Evaluation Form" (ms, 21 August 1981), folder 16, all in box 9, Country School Legacy Collection.

22.   Diane Ravitch, *The Troubled Crusade: American Education, 1945–1980* (New York: Basic Books, 1983), 312; William J. Reese, *America's Public Schools: From the Common School to 'No Child Left Behind'* (Baltimore: Johns Hopkins University Press, 2005), 217; Patrick J. Buchanan, "The Next Great Taxpayer Raid," 10 September 1991, at http://Buchanan .org/blog/p=147, accessed 17 August 2007.

23.   Gerald J. Stout, *Requiem for the Little Red Schoolhouse* (Athol, Mass.: Athol Press, 1987), 111, 120; *The Little Country Schoolhouse* (Berne, Ind.: House of White Birches, 1996), p. 9, "Introduction: General History and Non-Michigan Schools" binder, Britton Collection; *School Days* (Greendale, Wisc.: Reminisce Books, n.d. [1999]), 42; Bruno Bettelheim, "'Our Children Are Treated Like Idiots,'" *Psychology Today* 15 (July 1981): 38, 34.

24.   Bettelheim, "'Our Children Are Treated Like Idiots,'" 38; Isabel M. Hoy, "Seminar Evaluation Form" (ms, 18 September 1981), folder 21, box 9, Country School Legacy Collection; Laura E. Yowell, "Lessons from the One-Room School," *Delta Kappa Gamma Bulletin* (22 August 1994): p. 50, "Introduction: General History and Non-Michigan Schools" binder; William Pless, "Reminisces of a Childhood" (ms, n.d.), p. 44; "Gage-Glidden" binder; Helen Wiegmink to Bess Britton, n.d. [1993], "Volume A" binder, all in Britton Collection.

25.   *Putnam County, Ohio, One-Room Schools* (Kalida: Putnam County Historical Society, 1985), 99; Herbert A. Ellison, *The Old One-Room Country School* (Aurora, Colo.: National Writers Press, 1996), 43; J. K. White to Andrew Gulliford, 19 December 1980, folder 29, box 10, Country School Legacy Collection; *Good Old Days Remembers the Little Country Schoolhouse*, ed. Ken Tate and Janice Tate (Berne, Ind.: House of White Birches, 1999), 133.

26.   George E. Webb, *The Evolution Controversy in America* (Lexington: University Press of Kentucky, 1994), 217; Robert A. Peterson, "The Christian Influence on American Education: Forfeiting Our Forefathers' Foundation," *Fundamentalist Journal* 5 (September 1986): 14; *School Days*, 76; "One-Room Schoolhouse Surviving After 100 Years," *New York Times*, 15 December 1979.

27.   Council for American Private Education, *Facts and Studies* (2007), at

http://www.capenet.org/facts.html; Andrew Gulliford, *America's Country Schools*, 3rd ed. (Boulder: University Press of Colorado, 1996), 9; "No Obituaries, Yet, for One-Room Schools," *Wall Street Journal*, 7 March 1989; Edward S. Klimuska and Marty Heisey, *Amish One-Room Schools: Lessons for the Plain Life* (Lancaster, Pa.: Lancaster Newspapers, n.d. [1989]), 5, 11; "Flashcard," *New York Times*, 6 June 1989.

28. Mitchell L. Stevens, *Kingdom of Children: Culture and Controversy in the Homeschooling Movement* (Princeton: Princeton University Press, 2001), 10–11; Ron Strom, "Baptist Activists: Pull Kids out of School," *World Net Daily*, 4 May 2004, at http://www.worldnetdaily.com/news/article.asp?ARTICLE_ID=38322; "The Little Red Schoolhouse," at www.tviddy.com/school.htm; Monica Smatlak Liao, "Keeping Home: Home Schooling and the Practice of Conservative Protestant Identity" (Ph.D. diss., Vanderbilt University, 2006), 94.

29. Clay Miller, "Learning the Hard Way," *Progressive Architecture* 72 (March 1992): supp., p. 7; Amy Weisser, "Whither the Little Red Schoolhouse?," *Progressive Architecture* 72 (March 1992): supp., p. 33; Robin Fogarty, "The Little Red Schoolhouse," in *Think About . . . Multiage Classrooms: An Anthology of Original Essays*, ed. Robin Fogarty (Palantine, Il.: IRI/Skylight Training and Publishing, 1995), 5; *Recollections of a One-Room Schoolhouse: An Interview with Marian Brooks* (New York: City College School of Education, April 1975), 1; "Crowded Schools in Queens Find Class Space in Unusual Places," *New York Times*, 8 June 1994.

30. Anne C. Lewis, "Back to the One-Room School," *Washington Post*, 10 September 1978, folder 6; Clark McKinley, "One-Room School: Is Smaller Better?" *Rocky Mountain News*, 31 May 1981, folder 43, both in box 10, Country School Legacy Collection; *Country School Legacy: Humanities on the Frontier*, 53; "Big Grant to Oakland Education," *San Francisco Chronicle*, 15 November 2000; *Advocates for Community and Rural Education* 1 (30 April 2004), 1, at www.aracre.org; "Smaller Schools Promote a Friendlier Learning Climate," *NSBA School Board News* (5 December 2000), at www.nsba.org; William Celis 3rd, "In the Tiniest Places, Schools Big Cities Would Emulate," *New York Times*, 2 June 1996; Jodi Wilgoren, "The One-Room Schoolhouse," *New York Times*, 6 August 2000.

31. Rita Seedorf, *One Room Out West: The Story of the Jore Schoolhouse and Its Students* (Spokane: Eastern Washington University Press, 2002), 5–6; "Students Take Education Classes in Old Schoolhouse," *Kalamazoo Gazette*, 28 September 1997, "Benedict-Bond" binder, Britton Collection.

32. Kriste Lindberg and Annette Johnson Serrano, "The Blackwell History of Education Research Collection" (ms, n.d.), 5, 11; Blackwell History of Education Museum, *Country School Endowment Fund* (n.p., n.d.); Blackwell History of Education Museum, *The Milan Township District #83 Schoolhouse* (n.p., n.d.), all in General Collection, Blackwell History of Education Museum, DeKalb, Illinois.

33. The One-Room Schoolhouse Center, at http://www2.johnstown.k12.oh .us/cornell/states.html; Gerald J. Stout to Andrew Gulliford, 12 May 1981, folder 25, box 10, Country School Legacy Collection; *Lorna Grabe: Family History and the Story of the Soap Creek Schoolhouse Foundation*, interview by Bob Zyback, 28 December 1989 (Soap Creek Valley History Project, OSU Research Forests, Monograph no.1), pp. 63, 19, General Collection, Oregon State University Library, Corvallis; Manaseri, "Keeping School," 105; Elgin L. Klugh, "African-American Schoolhouses: Community, History, and Reclamation" (Ph.D. diss., University of South Florida, 2004), 277.

34. Klugh, "African-American Schoolhouses," 276; Tom Kelleher email message to author, 1 September 2006; Lori Ann Rider to Andrew Gulliford, 22 January 1985; Beth Floridie to Gulliford, 22 January 1985; Priscille Butenhoff to Gulliford, 20 January 1985, all in folder 23, box 10, Country School Legacy Collection; Mark L. Shanks, "Bringing the Schoolhouse to Life: Methodologies of Living History Education Demonstrated in a Living History Program for San Timoteo Schoolhouse, Riverside County, California" (M.A. diss., California State University San Bernardino, 1994), 119.

35. Richard Todd, "School of Thought," *Preservation* 55 (March–April 2003): 24–25; "School Ralph Nader Couldn't Save Is Razed," *New York Times*, 9 July 1988.

36. Joanne Raetz Stuttgen, "(Re)constructing the Little Red Schoolhouse: History, Landscape, and Memory" (Ph.D. diss, Indiana University, 2002), 148, 205–7, 228; "School's Out," newspaper clipping, n.d., n.p. [1993], "Introduction: General History and Non-Michigan Schools" binder, Britton Collection; "At the Nation's Table," *New York Times*, 25 October 1995; "Lox Is Key to School Sale," *New York Times*, 30 January 1977.

37. "School's Out"; "Making the Grade," *Kalamazoo Gazette*, 24 April 1995; "Couple Converts Old Schoolhouses into Homes," *Detroit News*, 24 July 1999; "Man Turns His Childhood School into Livable Home," newspaper clipping, n.p., 3 January 1999, all in "Introduction: General History and Non-Michigan Schools" binder, Britton Collection.

38. *National Register of Historic Places, 1966 to 1994* (Washington, D.C.: Preservation Press, 1994), xiv; National Trust for Historic Preservation, "11 Most Endangered Places: Historic Neighborhood Schools," at http://www.nationaltrust.org/11most/list.asp?i-29, accessed 7 August 2007; Richard Moe, "Don't Abandon Historic Schools," *USA Today*, 7 September 2000, reprinted in *The Slate* 7 (Fall/Winter 2000): pp. 3, 6, "*The Slate* binder"; Margaret Mullin, "The One-Room School" (ms, 1994), enclosed with Mullin to Bess Britton, 15 September 1994, "Introduction: General History and Non-Michigan Schools" binder, both in Britton Collection.

39. Gulliford, *America's Country Schools*, 11; One-Room Schoolhouse Center; Carolyn Kitch, *Pages from the Past: History and Memory in American Magazines* (Chapel Hill: University of North Carolina Press, 2005), chap. 6; *My Folks and the One-Room Schoolhouse: A Treasury of One-Room School Stories Shared by Capper's Readers* (Topeka, Kan.: Capper Press, 1993), iii.

40. "Schoolhouse Search Goes On," newspaper clipping, n.p., n.d., enclosed with John Hall to Andrew Gulliford, n.d., folder 3, box 11, Country School Legacy Collection; "Assignment for Photographer: Keep Old School Days in Focus," *Country Woman* (September–October 1998): p. 49, "Introduction: General History and Non-Michigan Schools" binder, Britton Collection.

41. Stuttgen, "(Re)constructing the Little Red Schoolhouse," 211; *My Folks and the One-Room Schoolhouse*, 20, 26; *Good Old Days Remembers*, 63; "Coughran School Reunion Celebrated in a 'Big Way,'" *Fowlerville* (Mich.) *News and Views*, 24 August 1992; Betty Ruth Yago Smyth, "A Teacher Remembers" (ms, February 1992), p. 8, both in "Code-Cushing" binder, Britton Collection.

CONCLUSION

Dear Old Golden Rule Days?

1. Michael F. Anderson, "Foreword," in *Under One Roof: A Traveler's Guide to America's One-Room Schoolhouse Museums*, ed. Grace S. Schoerner (Pine, Ariz.: Pine-Strawberry Archaeological Society, 2000), xi, xviii.

2. Edna M. Hill, "The Little Red Schoolhouse a 'Fake,'" *Independent* (7 August 1913): 318; *Country School Legacy: Humanities on the Frontier* (Silt, Colo.: Country School Legacy, 1981), 6; Paul Theobald, *Call School:*

Rural Education in the Midwest to 1918 (Carbondale: Southern Illinois University Press, 1995), 132; *The Rural Schools of San Luis Obispo County, 1850–1975—The End of the One Room School Era* (San Luis Obispo, Calif.: San Luis Obispo Superintendent of Schools, 1975), folder 10, box 21, Country School Legacy Collection, University Archives, University of Colorado Libraries, Boulder; Andrew Gulliford, *America's Country Schools*, 3rd ed. (Boulder: University Press of Colorado, 1996), 159–95.

3. Michael Kammen, *Mystic Chords of Memory: The Transformation of Tradition in American Culture* (New York: Vintage, 1993), 694; Janelle L. Wilson, *Nostalgia: Sanctuary of Meaning* (Lewisburg, Pa.: Bucknell University Press, 2005), 45–46; Barry Schwartz, *George Washington: The Making of an American Symbol* (Ithaca, N.Y.: Cornell University Press, 1990); Schwartz, *Abraham Lincoln and the Forge of National Memory* (Chicago: University of Chicago Press, 2003).

4. Anne C. Lewis, "Back to the One-Room School," *Washington Post*, 10 September 1978, folder 6, box 10, Country School Legacy Collection; Elma Streeter, "School Days 75 Years Ago" (ms, n.d. [1991?]), p. 4, "C-Cobtown" binder, Bess Britton Michigan One-Room Schoolhouse Collection, Van Buren District Library, Decatur, Michigan; *Readin' 'Ritin' 'Rithmetic and Reminiscin': A Bicentennial Project by the Iowa Retired Teachers Association* (n.p.: Iowa Retired Teachers Association, 1976), 90.

5. Carl Kaestle, *Pillars of the Republic: Common Schools and American Society, 1780–1860* (New York: Hill and Wang, 1983), 18; Jane Kenyon, "Trouble with Math in a One-Room Country School" (1986), in *Learning by Heart: Contemporary American Poetry About School* (Iowa City: University of Iowa Press, 1999), 101.

6. Mabel Anthony, *I Remember When: In and Around South Haven* (n.p., n.d. [1996?]), p. 6, "M" binder, Britton Collection; George T. Martin, *The Evolution of the Massachusetts Public School System* (New York: Appleton, 1894), 109.

7. Anthony, *I Remember When*, 40; Jeanne Hallgren, "Casco Township, Bounty by the Lake—The History of Casco Township, Allegan County, Michigan, 1844–1995" (ms, 1996), p. 41, "M" binder, Britton Collection.

8. "Can Burlesque Succeed on Broadway—After 50 Years?" *New York Times*, 7 October 1979; Guinevere Koppler, "Crime and Punishment," 133; John Slobodnik, "I Was a Bad Boy," 130, both in *Good Old Days Remembers the Little Country Schoolhouse*, ed. Ken Tate and Janice Tate

(Berne, Ind.: House of White Birches, 1999); *School Days* (Greendale, Wisc.: Reminisce Books, n.d. [1999]), title page.

9. David Lowenthal, *The Past Is a Foreign Country* (Cambridge: Cambridge University Press, 1985), 4; Svetlana Boym, *The Future of Nostalgia* (New York: Basic Books, 2001), xiv; Nicholas D. Kristof, "4 Teacher's Pets," *New York Times*, 1 November 2003; "Back to the One-Room School," *Good Old Days* (September 1993): p. 23; Robert Hastings, "When Schools Had Fewer Frills," *LifeTimes* (October 1995): p. 12, both in "Introduction: General History and Non-Michigan Schools" binder, Britton Collection.

10. Joyce Carol Oates, "Nostalgia" (1996), in *Learning by Heart*, 68; Oates, *A Garden of Earthly Delights* (1967; New York: Modern Library, 2003, at https://www.randomhouse.com/modernlibrary/oates.html).

11. Lowenthal, *Past Is a Foreign Country*, 8; Sandy Scofield to Andrew Gulliford, 14 July 1981, folder 16, box 9, Country School Legacy Collection; Nancyann Rell, "Childhood Memories Come Alive," *Daily Argus* (Mount Vernon, N.Y.), 25 January 1981, "Little Red Schoolhouse—Memoirs, Historical Articles" folder, box 5, Little Red Schoolhouse Collection, Special Collections, Lehman College Library, the Bronx, New York.

12. Andrew Gulliford, "The One-Room School Lives!" *Principal* 65 (September 1985): pp. 9, 6, folder 27, box 9, Country School Legacy Collection; "The One-Room School Is Saved in Nebraska," *New York Times*, 23 November 1986; "Long Time A' Coming," *Omaha World-Herald*, 5 June 2005.

13. Michael P. Riccards, *The Myth of American Mis-Education: A Popular Guide to Reform* (New York: Global Scholarly Publications, 2004), 6; "Voucher Program Front and Center," *St. Petersburg Times*, 21 May 2000; "Cabinet Member Assails Reagan Stance on Education," *New York Times*, 2 May 1980; "Reagan Steps Up Partisan Attack," *New York Times*, 8 February 1984.

14. Ben Sargent, "School days," United Press Syndicate, 13 April 1998, at http://www.amureprints.com/Detail.asp?ImageID=68667; Mike Keefe, "Lunatic Alert Level," *Denver Post*, 4 October 2006, at http://www.politicalcartoons.com.

Index

Index

U.S. Department of Agriculture, 82
U.S. Department of Education, 1–2, 182
USIA (United States Information Agency), 98, 100
U.S. Office of Education, 102
Utah, 37

Vachon, John, 97
Vaudeville, 70–71
Vermont: education in, during 1960s and 1970s, 138; funding for schools in, 92–93; historical pageant in, 92–93; number of one-room schools in, 25, 139; open schools in, 139; penknife drawings in schools in, 26; teaching aids in schools in, 25
Virginia: school integration in, 120; school overcrowding in, 121; standards for schools in, 47; students' retaliation against teacher in, 36
Vouchers, 181–82

Waltons, 143
Ward, Edward J., 59, 89–90
War on Poverty, 134
Warren, L. D., 120
Washington, George, 26, 172
Washington State, 72

Webster, Daniel, 38
White House Conference on Natural Beauty, 147
White House conference on rural education (1944), 116
Whitman, Walt, 62, 65, 94
Whittier, John Greenleaf, 60–61, 64, 69, 147, 151, 179
Wilder, Laura Ingalls, 109–11, 119, 143, 156
Windows of one-room schools, 23, 47
Wisconsin: Bennett Law (1889) in, 76–77, 80; number of one-room schools in, 17; opposition to one-room schools in, 87; outhouses for one-room schools in, 27; photograph of schoolchildren in, 107; political campaigns in, 76–77
Wisconsin v. Yoder, 154–55
Wolcott, Marion Post, 97–98, 104–7
Wood, Grant, 114–15
Works Progress Administration (WPA), 102–3, 108, 112
World War II, 4, 99–100, 115–18
WPA (Works Progress Administration), 102–3, 108, 112
Wyoming, education in, during 1980s and 1990s, 152

Yale Literary Magazine, 63